SEEING THROUGH THE FOG

SEEING THROUGH THE FOG

HOPE WHEN YOUR WORLD FALLS APART

ED DOBSON

SEEING THROUGH THE FOG
Published by David C Cook
4050 Lee Vance View
Colorado Springs, CO 80918 U.S.A.

David C Cook Distribution Canada
55 Woodslee Avenue, Paris, Ontario, Canada N3L 3E5

David C Cook U.K., Kingsway Communications
Eastbourne, East Sussex BN23 6NT, England

The graphic circle C logo is a registered trademark of David C Cook.

The website addresses recommended throughout this book are offered as a
resource to you. These websites are not intended in any way to be or imply an
endorsement on the part of David C Cook, nor do we vouch for their content.

Unless otherwise noted, all Scripture quotations are taken from the Holy
Bible, New International Version®, NIV®. Copyright © 1973, 1984, 2011
by Biblica, Inc.™ Used by permission of Zondervan. All rights reserved
worldwide. www.zondervan.com. Other Scripture quotations are taken
from the King James Version of the Bible. (Public Domain); and the
New Revised Standard Version Bible (NRSV), copyright 1989, Division of
Christian Education of the National Council of the Churches of Christ in
the United States of America. Used by permission. All rights reserved.

LCCN 2012943545
ISBN 978-0-7814-0555-3
eISBN 978-1-4347-0517-4

© 2012 Ed Dobson

The Team: Alex Field, Andy Meisenheimer, Karen Elmendorf,
Amy Konyndyk, Jack Campbell, Karen Athen
Cover Design and Illustration: Nick Lee

Printed in the United States of America
First Edition 2012

1 2 3 4 5 6 7 8 9 10

071712

To Lorna,
my wife and a pilgrim on the journey with me

CONTENTS

FOREWORD

Before You Begin ...

I need stories like this one.

Even though I've lived forty-five years with quadriplegia, my disability doesn't make me an expert on dealing with suffering. To be honest, were it not for God's Word and gutsy fellow-warriors like Ed Dobson, I would have emotionally crumbled long ago. Life is hard and I *need* stories of inspiration. I need to see others persevere through pain—and do so courageously. I need to absorb the life experiences of fellow journeymen who have put the Bible to the test and found that the grace of God *is* sufficient.

I think you're the same way. Life is wired to be difficult and, for the most part, it takes everything we've got to handle it with grace. And when one bad thing piles on top of the next, it can tip the balance. Then you wake up in the morning only to discover you've lost every bright prospect for a better day.

That's no way to live. And that's why this book is so powerful. It's about finding the "better day" of *real* hope. Not hope as wishful thinking or an aspiration for easier times. *Seeing through the Fog* goes deeper than that. Its message is far more profound than "wishing upon a star." This incredible story illustrates that hope is rock-solid and real, unshakable, immovable, and most of all *eternal*.

My friend Ed understands that heartfelt trust in God is within reach even when—*especially* when—your prospects for a brighter day completely unravel. The first chapter starts out, in fact, with a diagnosis: "Ed, you have ALS. You have three to five years to live." How do you *live* when you receive such devastating news? How do you wake up in the morning and still want to go on?

Ed is blazing that path. And in the pages of this book, he shows us just how *high* a little hope can lift a hurting heart. *Seeing through the Fog* points to how *potent* hope is. Like a small candle glowing in a dark room—the flame is so tiny and the room is so big, yet light from even the smallest candle dispels darkness.

So I thank my friend Ed Dobson for reminding us how to hold on to hope as though it were the thin string of a big kite—the string is so thin in your hand, yet it connects to a force that can almost lift you off the ground. Ed shows us that this is the only way to live—hope in God is the best choice for happiness and blessing. To hope in God is to rely on Him when all else fails, because you know His mercies and compassion are fresh toward you every day. To hope in God means assurance that one day all sorrow and sadness will disappear, and you will have a home in heaven.

Does it mean this story has the "happy ending" of no more ALS? No more Lou Gehrig's disease? No. It conveys something far better. The life and struggles of Ed Dobson underscore that a diseased-ravaged body does not have to be a deterrent when it comes to trusting God—rather, it can be what pushes us into the arms of the God of all hope.

And I think Ed would agree, that beats walking any day.

Joni Eareckson Tada
Fall 2012

ACKNOWLEDGMENTS

Over the years, I have written dozens of books. I have always had a reputation for delivering them on time to the publisher. This book is the exception to that standard. I have missed deadline after deadline after deadline. I'm really not sure why. Maybe it's because I know this is one of the last books I will ever write. Maybe it's because the topic of ALS is so painful for me. Maybe it's because writing this book stirs up all of the emotions I've felt over the years.

Anyway, thanks to Don Pape and Alex Field at David C Cook for being patient with me. And thanks to Andy and Mandy Meisenheimer for their help with the book and for pushing me to finish. Without their input and advice, this book would never have been written.

INTRODUCTION

I grew up in Belfast, Northern Ireland, and when I wanted to go somewhere, I took a city bus. Back in those days, most of the buses were double-deckers. When I'd get on the bus, I would go up the stairs and sit in the front row. I felt like I was in command of the bus. I could see everything. Both sidewalks, both sides of shops and buildings. Both lines of traffic. The traffic light ahead. It was exhilarating. I could see it all.

One day I was riding the bus when the fog rolled in. In Belfast, the fog can be extremely thick. This time, it was so thick that the driver of the bus had someone walk next to the bus to make sure he didn't bump into anything. As I sat there, I couldn't see sidewalks, shops, buildings, traffic, lights, nothing. I felt that I was no longer in control. I was controlled by the fog.

And that's how it feels when you have ALS.

Before ALS, you see everything clearly. You think you're in control. Once ALS hits, you see nothing clearly. And you know for sure you're not in control.

This is a book about hope. Not the kind of hope that *ignores* your current circumstances. Not the kind of hope that *goes around* your current circumstances. Not the kind of hope that *dismisses* your current circumstances. But the kind of hope that can come only *in the midst of* your circumstances.

It's a hope that comes with strength: the strength to keep living life, despite its challenges, and to continually give thanks for the blessings we have, even in the darkest of times. When faced with a terminal illness, knowing that your life will slowly deteriorate over time, this all is much easier said than done. Hopefully you'll see that in this book. I have struggled the past eleven years to keep going, to have hope that I can still live while I am alive, that I am buried but not yet dead.

This is a battle I fight nearly every day.

I have learned that we all will struggle in life. There are no exceptions. It might be cancer. It might be divorce. It might be the loss of a child. It might be brokenness. It might be depression. Whatever it is, we all struggle with something. That's part of what it means to be human. The question then becomes, how can I find hope when I am in the middle of struggle? That's what this book is about. And it does not offer easy answers. There is no verse from the Bible to explain what makes it all go away. There is no prayer that makes it all go away. This book does not offer three points that will revolutionize your experience. This book is about my personal journey. I pray that in reading about my experience, you will find hope and strength for your journey as well.

My struggle with ALS began in the fall of 2000, when I was diagnosed. ALS (amyotrophic lateral sclerosis, also known as Lou Gehrig's disease) is a disease where the neurons in your nerves die. Consequently, the electrical impulses from your brain fail to reach your muscles. And then the muscles die as well. Researchers do not know what causes this disease, and there is no cure. For five years I took an FDA-approved drug that was thought to extend your life by three months. After five years I decided to quit taking the medication. Since ALS causes your muscles to die, it's a degenerative disease; it gets worse and worse over time. There are no times when it stabilizes. There are no times when it is reversed. ALS is a downward spiral, month after month. It is a fatal, terminal disease. When I was diagnosed, doctors gave me two to five years to live and said most of that time I would be in a disabled condition.

I have never been afraid of dying, but I was very concerned about the process of getting there. Initially, I sank into a fog of despair about my future. It took me months to really begin to come out of it. Along the way, I learned some great lessons. All humans suffer. And there is a common denominator to our suffering. I hope and sincerely pray that what I have learned through facing ALS is also helpful to those who are experiencing different kinds of suffering.

1

THE DIAGNOSIS

My first recollection of something being wrong was on my fiftieth birthday, December 30. I was at a funeral home, meeting with the deceased's family so I could conduct the memorial service. Aside from planning specific details about the service, this meeting also gave me the opportunity to get to know the deceased in a better way. As I sat in a circle with the family, I was busy taking notes. The entire time I was with this family, my eyelid was twitching. I would rub it, but it made no difference. I would blink hard, but to no avail. The entire time I wrote notes, my eyelid was twitching. I thought, *Well, this is what you get when you turn fifty!*

Fortunately, when I left the funeral home, my eyelid stopped twitching. But then the twitching spread. I noticed it when I lay down in bed at night—muscles throughout my entire back were twitching. Even my wife noticed it, and she encouraged me to go see the doctor. I agreed with her, but I never made an appointment.

Months later it was summer, and every August for the past several years, I would go backpacking for a week with about twenty high school students in Manistee National Forest in northern Michigan. We would take students about to enter their senior year in high school and spend a week with them, getting to know them better. It was one of the weeks I looked forward to most every year.

Backpacking is brilliant. Everything you need, you put in the backpack. Once you enter the woods, you are on your own. If the tent leaks, you fix it. If the cooking stove doesn't work, you fix it. I love it. For most of the students, it is their first time backpacking. The first few days they are really nervous. But gradually they adjust. They carry their own

HIKING

Ten years before I was diagnosed, Lorna and I were at a ministry conference in northern Michigan, something we had done for the past eight years, and this one woman in our group said, "What are you going to do when your kids are gone?" And it was then that we started thinking about what it is that we like to do.

Lorna said, "Well, we could walk," and I took that to mean hiking. I bought an encyclopedia of walking, then started buying all sorts of cooking magazines and books about gourmet cooking while you're on the trail, and I had three backpacks and so many tents: winter, lightweight, medium weight. I had all the gear.

We had a really bad experience camping once when my oldest was eleven; the food wasn't so good, and more than half of us got wet during the night, and Lorna said she wasn't going to go again unless I learned how to camp properly from a guy in our church who knew about survival.

backpacks. They set up their own tents. They cook their own food. They dig their own toilets. If it is hot, it is hot. If it rains, it rains. We are at the mercy of the elements, the trail, and each other.

But this year, I realized I was having a few problems. I was having trouble opening jars. I was having trouble pumping the handle on the water purifier and actually found it tiring, which was unusual. My backpack seemed heavier than in years past. In fact, on the third day I allowed a few students to carry some of my stuff, which I had never done before.

But just as I had done the previous December, I chalked it all up to the idea that this is simply what happens when you turn fifty.

One morning in early October, I was writing out my sermon notes when something strange happened. I had this sensation that my mind and my hands were not completely coordinated. It was as if my hand was a second behind my brain. Now, for the first time, I was truly concerned. That Sunday, like always, I sat in the front row during the service. Right behind me was a neurologist friend with whom I had played golf on many occasions. During the congregational song right before I was to preach, I turned around to him.

"When I was writing my notes this week, I had a strange feeling that my mind and my hand were not coordinated. Also, I've been having difficulty opening jars when I backpack. What do you think that is?" (As if this doctor was going to diagnose me during the morning service on Sunday!)

"I think you better come see me—like, tomorrow."

I made an appointment the following day. The neurologist examined each of my muscle groups, at times holding my hands and having me push or pull in certain directions.

Then I went into his office to talk with him.

"There are several possibilities of what is going on here," he said. "First, your twitches could be benign fasciculation. That's twitching. Everyone twitches."

"So I could just be a big twitcher. I can live with that."

"On the other hand, it might be ALS."

ALS? That was much worse than being a twitcher. My head became foggy. It was as if everything around me slowed down. I could hardly hear anything else the doctor said as he explained what exactly amyotrophic lateral sclerosis is.

As I sat there in his office, I remembered two people at Calvary Church who had died of ALS and wondered if I would share their fate.

The first was a young man named Caleb, who was diagnosed shortly after I became pastor. He was only twenty years old and had been a star athlete who excelled in racquetball, pole vaulting, and other athletics during his high school and early college years.

For seven years I walked with him during his journey with the disease.

I played golf with Caleb while he was able to walk. The last time we played, his legs were so wobbly that when he hit off the tee, I thought for sure he was going to fall over. He also insisted on driving the cart, which increased my prayer life. Once his legs failed him, we took to playing video games at times—he had a flight-simulator game where you could pretend to fly a Cessna around Chicago. He handed me the controller once and told me to give it a try. I got the plane off the ground but then turned around and around and couldn't find the airport to land. For some reason he laughed and laughed that I couldn't find the airport. He took the controller with his weakened arms and hands and within seconds had the plane back on the ground.

As he continued his downward spiral, I tried to visit with him every month. I remember the day he told me he had reached a major decision.

"There's something I want you to see," he said. "I am going to print something off the computer, and then I want you to read it. But I want you to read the whole thing before you comment."

So I sat there in silence reading what Caleb had written. He had decided that seven years was enough with ALS. He had made the decision that beginning the following week, he would refuse food. He asked me what I thought.

"Well, you are in the process of dying, one muscle at a time. This is irreversible. By refusing food, you are simply speeding up that process. So I think I would support you in your choice not to take food."

He smiled. And this kid had one of the greatest smiles I have ever seen. I realized how much I would miss seeing it on his face. I visited him many times in the hospital while he refused food. It was painful to see him in that condition, but I decided that it was his choice and that I would support him. Not everyone felt the same way; in fact, many of his good friends turned against him in those final days.

The second man I thought of as I sat in the doctor's office that October day was Fred, a successful farmer in his sixties. One day Fred was riding in a golf cart, and when the driver made a sharp turn, Fred fell out. A series of doctor visits stemming from that accident eventually resulted in the diagnosis that he had ALS. Fred's health deteriorated quickly. I frequently visited him on his farm, often helping him exercise his muscles to avoid cramping. When Fred lost the ability to speak, he would shine a light attached to his glasses on various letters on an alphabet card to slowly form words. I was with him the night before he died. On that final night, he used that alphabet card to express nothing but love for his family, who were at his side when he passed.

So as I was sitting there in the doctor's office, I could see Caleb and Fred in my mind. But as I saw them, they were in their worst conditions. And I thought, *Is that me? Is that my future?*

"There are some tests that I can do," the doctor said. "But if I were you, I would go to the University of Michigan ALS clinic and let them run the tests." He also told me that it would likely be a month before I could get into the clinic. A month of waiting in a fog of uncertainty.

So I agreed to go to the clinic. My mind was racing in a million directions. The doctor walked me to the door saying he would set me up with the U of M neurology clinic and told me to call him when I got the results. When I walked outside, the sun was shining. The leaves were beginning to turn. It was one of those incredible October afternoons. As I got into my truck, I realized that my world had been turned upside down. Nothing would ever be the same again.

I sat there in the truck for a long time, alone. I remembered a trip to Israel years ago. Just outside Jerusalem is the ancient site of Bethany. If you walk down one of the back roads, you will come to a sign that says "The Tomb of Lazarus." After paying a man several shekels and ducking under a doorway, you encounter a spiral stone staircase that goes down and down and down. When you get to the bottom, you have to crawl under a large stone. Once you crawl under that stone, you are in an authentic second-temple-period burial chamber, with walls lined with shelves for stacking the bodies of the deceased. It's dark. It's cold. It's musty. It's claustrophobic. It feels like death. It is far from the laughter of children and the sunshine above.

Sitting in my truck, I felt like I was underground in that tomb again. And three little letters sent me down that spiral stone staircase—ALS. I didn't know what to do!

The easiest thing would be to lie down on one of those shelves used for the bodies and just wait for death. But do I really want to give up? Do I really want to lie down and die?

The month of waiting that followed that first appointment was terrible. On some days I was absolutely convinced beyond any shadow of a doubt that I had ALS. On other days I wholly believed that I didn't have any of the symptoms of ALS. The uncertainty of those days drove me crazy. If I just knew my diagnosis, one way or another, at least then I could move on with my life.

The Internet can be a wonderful way to research medical conditions. I accessed many different sites that month, accumulating a vast layman's knowledge of ALS. I soon discovered that one of the problems with ALS is that it is very difficult to diagnose. Doctors actually look at all the other possible explanations for a patient's situation, and if none of them work out, then ALS becomes the default diagnosis. I also visited chat rooms for ALS patients. I think those were the most helpful because I was talking to real people who had the disease, and they understood what I was facing.

Continuing to work during that month of waiting was probably the biggest and strangest challenge of all. I still had to study and prepare sermons. I still had to make visits to the sick. I still had to conduct weddings. I still had to conduct funerals. I still had staff meetings to attend. I still had to preach every Sunday. And through all of these daily activities, which I have always felt so blessed to do, I experienced an underlying sense of doom. Sometimes in the middle of my preaching, I wanted to just stop and tell the congregation what was really going on. Sometimes while counseling others, I wanted to stop and discuss what was happening to me. It seemed to me that their problems were not as significant as mine. While visiting people undergoing cancer treatments, I would think, *Well at least you have the possibility of a cure. I don't.* I didn't do any of those things, thank goodness. But just getting out of bed every day, showering, getting dressed, eating breakfast, and going to work was a huge challenge for me while the cloud of uncertainty loomed overhead.

Finally the day came for my follow-up appointment at the University of Michigan ALS clinic. It was the week before Thanksgiving. My wife, Lorna, and I left the house early in the morning to make the two-hour drive to Ann Arbor. As I drove, my heart was pounding. I knew that something serious was going on, that this was going to be a big day. But I didn't know what that meant. We stopped at one of our favorite bars near the hospital to get lunch. I tried to eat what would normally be a delicious meal, but I just wasn't hungry. A good beer probably would've done me good that day, but I stuck to water.

At the hospital, we parked the car and began our walk through the vast hospital complex toward the ALS clinic. After registering and taking a seat in the waiting room, I noticed a man sitting in a wheelchair. His pale face and wispy gray hair sat atop a thin, tall frame. His arms and legs were motionless beneath his sweat suit. His hands occasionally twitched, and he used one of them to operate the chair. My heart sank as I realized I was looking at my future if I received a diagnosis of ALS that day.

The wait was agonizing, but eventually we were ushered into a small room to wait for the doctors. Several doctors came in; perhaps some were residents or students. They began by taking my medical history and wanted to know my recent symptoms. Then one of the doctors began testing all of my muscle groups, just as my neurologist friend had done the previous month. I tried to read their expressions to see if they could already tell I had ALS. But they were all poker-faced. They had me go out in the hall and walk the length of it on my heels, then return on my toes.

After this examination, they sent me for blood work to get a better picture of my overall health and to check for other ailments. Sitting and waiting for the blood work, I experienced a moment of encouragement. Several children were also in the lab, waiting to get their blood drawn. As sad as it was to think of what might be ailing those children, for the first time I also felt grateful. I realized that I had been blessed with fifty good years of healthy life.

After the blood work was over, the clinic sent me for EMG needle testing in another part of the clinic. After checking in, we were taken to a small room where I was asked to lie down on an examination table. So I lay on the table, looking up at the ceiling and counting the number of lights up there, trying to think of anything except where I was and why. Several doctors stood around me, and next to them were some computer monitors.

"What we are going to do is put some needles in your muscles, move them around slightly, and then measure what's happening in the muscle," the head of the ALS clinic said to me. "Just try to stay relaxed."

Stay relaxed? How in the world can you relax when people are sticking needles in your muscles? The doctor smiled and stuck in the first needle. The only word that comes to mind to describe this procedure is *nasty*. I did okay until they put the needle in my thumb muscle and began to move it around. At that point, the word *nasty* did not seem to do justice to what I was feeling. But I kept looking up at those lights, and after about twenty minutes, the testing was over at last. We were then sent back to the ALS clinic where the doctor would meet with us and go over all the testing.

"ALS is a very difficult disease to diagnose," the doctor said. "There are three categories of diagnosis. One: possible ALS. Two: probable ALS. Three: confirmed diagnosis. Now, your blood work came back as a normal. The needle testing showed that there is some damage in your right hand and arm but not in the other muscle groups. So we need to have your local neurologist do an

MRI to see if there are any difficulties in your spine. If that MRI comes back normal, then it is our suspicion that you have probable ALS."

That was it. All of the testing and all of the expertise of the doctors at this special ALS clinic led them to believe that I had "probable ALS."

I wanted them to tell me either I had ALS or I did not.

I did not want to endure any more waiting or uncertainty.

The doctors did give me a packet of information about ALS. In that packet, it said patients with probable ALS typically have two to five years to live following diagnosis, and most of that time would be in a disabled condition.

The drive home that day was surreal. As Lorna drove, I made phone calls to my children—one was still in high school, one in college, and my oldest was married and working at a church—to inform them of what the doctors had said. Most of the way, we drove in silence. I felt like I was sinking into the darkness and fog. I felt like my life was over. I felt like I had been buried alive. Once again I felt like I was in the tomb.

I couldn't sleep the night after my probable diagnosis. As I lay awake in bed, I felt every twitch in my muscles, and with each one

I felt closer to the end. My whole life played out before my eyes, especially my earliest memories of life in Northern Ireland and coming to America.

The night I left Ireland is one of those memories that will be etched in my mind forever. We left on a boat to Scotland, then the train to Southampton, England, and then aboard the *Queen Elizabeth* to America. The night we sailed from Belfast, more than nine hundred people were gathered on the dock. As the boat pulled away and I stood there on the deck with my mom, dad, and sister, the crowd began to sing:

> God be with you and till we meet again:
> by His counsel's guide, uphold you,
> with His sheep securely fold you;
> God be with you till we meet again.
> Till we meet, till we meet,
> till we meet at Jesus' feet;
> till we meet, till we meet,
> God be with you till we meet again.

Scanning the crowd on the dock, I noticed one of my best friends, Billy, waving the school scarf. Whenever I hear that tune, even today, it brings back the memories of that night in Belfast. I am still unable to sing the words of that song in any setting. It's too emotional. It's too dramatic.

Then I thought about the day we arrived in America. The captain told us that we would arrive in New York at about 4:30

in the morning. So my family and I woke early and stood at the back of the *Queen Elizabeth* as it pulled into New York City. I was overwhelmed by the size of the buildings. It seemed like they went on forever. I was overwhelmed at the size of American cars. Everything seemed bigger in America. On the way to our temporary home in South River, New Jersey, we stopped at Howard Johnson's for our first meal in America. I ordered a hot dog. I wanted to be American in every way!

As I thought about moving from Northern Ireland, I began to realize that I was facing a similar situation with ALS. When we left Ireland, we said good-bye to all of our family and friends. And then I knew eventually I would have to say good-bye to all of the family at Calvary Church. And I knew I would somehow have to say good-bye to my family members.

Then I started worrying about the future. What would life be like for my wife? Who would take care of her? What about my kids? What would happen to my job as a minister? Can I handle life in a wheelchair? What about breathing assistance? Would I have a feeding tube?

The questions kept coming through the sleepless night, and they all remained unanswered.

Finally morning came. I got up, dressed, ate breakfast, and went to work.

It was the first day of the remainder of my life.

2

THE FOG

For the past five or six years, I had been going to the Michigan Athletic Club to run every afternoon. The club had the best indoor track; it was somehow easier on the legs than other tracks I'd run on. The track was two lanes along the perimeter of the space, surrounding tennis courts that sat in the middle. Huge green curtains on the walls added warmth to the usually chilly building. The same people were often running on the track at the same time every day, so over the years I got to know quite a few of them.

Following my trip to the ALS clinic, I was not looking forward to seeing anyone on the track and didn't feel like running at all. But I knew it was important to exercise and a good thing for me to keep my normal routine while I could. I thought, *At least I can*

*do something today that I have always done. And that will be good
for me.*

As I ran around the track, I passed a woman whom I had lately
seen on my daily runs there. She had not been a runner for long,
I could tell, and was jogging rather slowly and panting for breath.

As I ran beside her, I asked, "How are you doing?"

"I'm dying," she replied.

Without hesitation I said, "Yep, me too!"

I laughed all the way around the track. It was the first time in
several weeks that I had laughed. And it felt good.

Preaching that first Sunday was difficult. I didn't feel like doing
it, but I really had no other choice. I recalled that the apostle Paul
gave Timothy some good advice: "Preach the word; be prepared
in season and out of season" (2 Timothy 4:2). In other words, we
are to preach the Word both when it is convenient and when it is
inconvenient. We are to preach the Word when we feel like it as
well as when we do not. That first Sunday was one of the times
when it was inconvenient and when I didn't feel like teaching the
Bible.

For the previous several months I had been teaching through
the gospel of Mark. When I preached through a book like that, I

didn't have a structured long-range plan; wherever I left off one week, I picked it up right there the next week. It just so happened that this particular Sunday, I was to preach on the story of Jesus walking on the water (Mark 6:45–51).

In this story, Jesus told His disciples to gather in a boat and to go to the other side of the Sea of Galilee, to Bethsaida. Meanwhile, Jesus went up on the mountainside to pray. While the disciples were out on the lake, a terrible storm rolled in. They struggled with all their might to get the boat to the shore. Then Jesus came to them in the middle of the sea by walking on the water. When the disciples saw Him, they thought He was a ghost. They cried out in terror. Immediately Jesus spoke to them and said, "Take courage! It is I. Don't be afraid." Then He climbed into the boat with them, and the wind died down. They were safe.

Preparing for that sermon, I quickly realized that I felt very much like the disciples. I had gotten into the boat (my boat being ministry at the church) because Jesus told me to do so. I was committed to Calvary Church. I had thoroughly enjoyed all the years God had given me there. I loved the people. I loved preaching. I loved seeing people grow. I was fifty years old. This was to be the decade of my greatest ministry. But now I was in the middle of a storm. I was about to sink in the wind and the waves.

I distinctly remember my points for that first sermon after my diagnosis. First, when you cannot see Jesus, He sees you. The text in Mark states that while Jesus was praying, He saw the disciples straining at the oars. Even though they could not see Him, He could see them. This is how I felt. I could not see Jesus, but deep down I knew that Jesus was with me and that He saw me. But it sure didn't feel that way. There was a great disparity between my theological knowledge and my personal experience. I could not see Jesus. But the wonderful thing was that He saw me. I had to keep reminding myself of that.

Second, when you cannot get to Jesus, He comes walking to you. Mark states that in the middle of the night, Jesus came to the disciples by walking on the water. Nothing could separate Jesus from His disciples or keep them apart. Not water, not a storm, not even death.

My last point was that when Jesus got into the boat, the wind stopped and the storm ceased. He brought peace. His very presence brought shalom to the sea and to the frightened passengers in that boat. That first Sunday, what I needed more than anything else was to have peace and shalom in my boat.

In one of the parallel accounts of this story, Peter said, "Lord, if it's you, tell me to come to you on the water" (Matthew 14:28). Jesus told him to come, and for a few moments, Peter did something that no other disciple had done—he walked on the water. Now, one of the desires of any Jewish disciple is to be just like his rabbi. A disciple wants to eat like the rabbi. He wants to walk like the rabbi. He wants to wash his hands like the rabbi. He wants to act exactly like the rabbi in every way; he believes in his rabbi's teachings that much. One interpretation of this story is that like any Jewish disciple, Peter wanted to be just like his rabbi, Jesus. So if Jesus could walk on water, Peter wanted to as well. So Peter got out of the boat to be like his teacher. For those first few steps, he believed he could do it.

As I thought about this story, I applied it to myself. If the wind and the waves represent ALS, then I know that Jesus can walk on water toward me, that He sees me in my struggle and can give me peace. But the question facing me then becomes, "Do I have faith to join Jesus and experience peace and shalom amid the storm?" In the days, weeks, and months following my diagnosis, I really didn't know. Of course I would like to walk on the water with Jesus, but I was so overwhelmed and worried that I was not sure I could get out of the boat ever again.

That first Sunday eventually arrived, and I preached my sermon at all three morning services. But really, I found I was preaching to myself. The first time through the sermon, at our early service, truthfully I wasn't sure I actually believed what I was saying. After my second time through the sermon, I began to believe that Jesus was watching me, was walking to me, offering me shalom, and encouraging me to get out of the boat. And by the end of the third sermon, I was overcome with great emotion and was on the verge of crying. I wanted so badly to share what I was facing, to exclaim, "I have just been diagnosed with ALS. I am in the middle of the biggest storm of my life, and I need your help!" But the time was not right, and I was not ready to share my struggle. After a few weeks, I did tell the congregation, but that first Sunday, I preached to myself and stood alone in my boat.

In looking back on that week of sermon preparation and my first Sunday with ALS, I realize that God was in control the whole time. Arriving at this text for that Sunday was His way of saying, "I see you, Ed. I'm walking to you. I'm in your boat. You can trust Me."

I have always enjoyed Thanksgiving. It is a uniquely American holiday. There is nothing like it in Northern Ireland, where I grew up. My first Thanksgiving in the United States was in South River, New Jersey. At that time we were living in the basement of a local church, thanks to the kindness of the pastor, Don Balfour, and his wife, Marie, who welcomed us to America and helped us adjust during our first month here. My parents slept in the pastor's study. My sister and I each slept in a Sunday school room. I remember mine: it contained a single bed in the corner, two tables surrounded by tiny chairs in the middle, and a flannelgraph board along the wall. It was my first bedroom in America, so I loved it.

Back then, I'm not sure I even knew the significance of Thanksgiving. All I knew was that we were having turkey for dinner, which was something we had only at Christmas in Ireland. Before dinner, my family and all the kids from the pastor's family played touch football in front of the church. This was my first introduction to American football; back in Ireland, "football" was soccer, which of course is quite a different game. The American kids explained the rules, and I just didn't get it: why was it called "football" if you don't use your feet? I was confused the whole game and was terrible at it. Finally, it was dinnertime. I was better at eating than at playing football. We sat around a large table in the church and ate together. We laughed. We talked. We gave thanks. It was great to be in America.

My first Thanksgiving with ALS was not as joyful as that first holiday so many decades before. Even though Lorna and I had all our kids together under one roof, and even though we had a wonderful meal, I could not enjoy a moment of it. My thoughts were consumed by ALS, my mind full of fear about facing my future. Each time I looked at my family, I was overcome with sadness and worry. The whole day was a nightmare; I struggled through the entire meal to keep my composure. I fought hard not to break down and cry. I wanted to be strong for the sake of my wife and kids, for I knew if they saw me fall apart, they would fall apart also. I wanted to appear brave, to show them that my recent diagnosis was not significantly impacting my life.

As I look back on that day, I wonder why people who have had the air knocked out of them try so hard to give the impression that it didn't hurt. Why do we put up such brave fronts? Why didn't I feel I could be honest with my family?

Despite the fact that I had not formally told the congregation of my diagnosis, the news began to spread. I call this phenomenon "the Christian gossip cycle." The speed at which bad news travels among Christians is infinitely quicker than the speed at which good news travels. I began to notice whispers around me and sympathetic expressions on faces each Sunday.

Soon after I realized the gossip was spreading, I walked into my office one day and sitting there by my desk was a large potted plant. It was huge, its leaves coming up to my waist. I thought, *Well, this is really wonderful. Someone has heard about my recent diagnosis and now they're sending me this beautiful plant.* I saw a card attached to one of the leaves, so I opened it. The plant was from a funeral home! I burst out laughing.

I rejoiced at the occasion to laugh; such moments had been scarce since the diagnosis. So laugh I did! A closer look at the card showed that the plant had nothing to do with my disease, as it was common for local funeral homes to send potted plants to ministers around Christmastime. I just happened to get one at an inopportune time.

December came, and I found myself sitting on our four-season porch one morning. I was all alone. Staring out the window, I watched as snow started to fall. As I sat there on the porch, various memories played out on the very lawn in front of me. I remembered setting up a winter tent with my children and watching them build forts and ski ramps out of piles of snow. I remembered springtime, kicking the soccer ball with my two sons and daughter, teaching them the game I so loved in my youth.

Then I felt my mind sinking, going to a familiar dark place. I thought, *This will be my last winter. This will be my last Christmas.* My thoughts kept descending. I admitted to myself that I was becoming depressed. I was spending too much time and energy in that dark tomb of despair. I didn't know what to do.

I was drawn to the speech Moses made shortly before he died: "This day I call the heavens and the earth as witnesses against you that I have set before you life and death, blessings and curses.

JESUS AS A MAN OF SORROW

I had always thought of Jesus as the resurrected Savior and Lord. And of course He is. He has conquered death and hell. He has ascended to the right hand of God. He is now the glorified and soon coming Savior. During all my years as a pastor, I had always thought of Jesus in those terms. Then I got ALS. And while I still believe that Jesus is all of the above, I now see Him as the suffering servant. Consider the words of the prophet Isaiah.

He was despised and rejected by mankind,
a man of suffering, and familiar with pain.
Like one from whom people hide their faces
he was despised, and we held him in low esteem.
Surely he took up our pain
and bore our suffering. (Isaiah 53:3–4)

>

> I had never thought much about Jesus being a man of sorrows. The notion always made sense to me, but it did not have much impact in my life. Then I got a terrible disease, and all of a sudden the idea of Jesus being sorrowful and carrying our pain made perfect sense to me.

Now choose life, so that you and your children may live" (Deuteronomy 30:19). Moses told the children of Israel that they had a choice: they could choose to live by obeying the Torah, or they could choose to die by disregarding it. The choice was theirs to make. As I sat there on the porch, for the first time I realized that I had a choice to make. I could choose to live, or I could choose to die. And the easier choice was to die. I could give up, lie down in the tomb, and await death. Or I could choose to keep living. So I prayed, "God, I want to live. Help me to make the choices that will help me to live."

That one prayer that I prayed on the porch was not sufficient to see me through to the end. I find that every day is a struggle between choosing to die and choosing to live. Every new day is a challenge that requires new strength. I've often prayed that prayer multiple times in a single day. I am determined to keep taking steps back toward the sunshine and toward the light.

3

CONNECTING
WITH OTHERS

I continued to run as often as I could during that first winter. After a workout one day, I spotted several guys in the hall who were watching people playing racquetball. As I passed by, one of them said, "I just heard that you have been diagnosed with ALS."

"Yes, I have."

"I have a brother who was diagnosed with ALS. He has had this for a number of years, and he is on a ventilator. Maybe you would like to go see him."

I definitely did not want to go see this man. Why would I want to visit someone who is much worse off than I am? I had only just begun wrapping my mind around what was to come for me; I did not want to be confronted with the misery that awaited me.

But I didn't say any of those things. Instead, I agreed to visit the man's brother, Robert.

I waited several weeks before I went to see him. At the hospital, I parked as far from the building as I could. I walked slowly to the entrance. Then I walked slowly to the unit where Robert was. Robert had been diagnosed with ALS a number of years ago after noticing his arms felt much weaker than usual. He had been an engineer. And now he was completely paralyzed with the exception of one eyebrow.

To communicate with Robert, I held up a card with the alphabet in rows. I would point to the first line on the card, and if the first letter of the word he wanted to communicate was in the line, he would raise his eyebrow. Then I would go down the line and when I got to the letter he wanted, he would raise his eyebrow again. Needless to say, communicating with him was a slow process. Initially, I would try to guess the word he was trying to say, but most of the time I was wrong.

That first visit, we spent several hours together. Robert told me he was going through a divorce. His wife was not happy with this decision to go on a ventilator, so they separated, and now she was asking for a divorce. It was a terrible situation.

After I left Robert's room that day and got on the elevator, I burst into tears. I could not fathom being totally paralyzed. I could not fathom being able to only raise one eyebrow. I could not fathom being on a ventilator. I could not fathom living my life in the hospital every day. I could not fathom my wife asking for a divorce. I could not fathom anything about Robert's situation.

I walked across the parking lot and got into my car. I sat there for the longest time thinking about Robert. What will I do when I am paralyzed? What will I do when I can only communicate slowly like that? What was I going to do when I ended up like him?

◆ ◆ ◆

Many months later, the local ALS chapter asked me if I would visit people who had the disease. Several weeks later, I went on my first visit. The husband of the woman with ALS met me at the door. He was short, like me, and had a long ponytail. He explained that he and his wife often watched the Calvary Church services on television.

The man shared with me his wife's journey thus far with ALS. When I asked if I could see her, the man went back into the bedroom to check. He returned with a frown and said, "Actually, right now she doesn't want to see you."

"Well, that's too bad. I'm going to see her anyway." And before the husband could react, I went to her bedroom. Before I was diagnosed, I would have told him that I would come back later and try to talk with her. Since being diagnosed, I have a greater sense of urgency and boldness.

The bedroom was small. It had a hospital bed in it and over in the corner a chest of drawers with a TV on top of it. She was lying on the bed, watching reruns of *Gunsmoke*. When I first introduced myself, she rolled over to face the wall with her back to me. I asked her a bunch of questions, but she never said a word in reply. In fact, she said nothing the entire time I was with her. Maybe she was mad at her husband for letting me in; maybe she was just mad because of the ALS. At the end of our visit, I prayed for her. When I left, she was still facing the wall with her back to me.

I went back many times to see the woman. And every time, when I walked into the bedroom, she would roll over and put her back to me. She never spoke. I didn't quite know what to do. So I ended up writing out a prayer for her: "As I face death and life beyond the grave, I am trusting Jesus as my Savior and Lord." I gave it to her husband, who put it up on the wall so every time she rolled over toward the wall she would see the prayer.

One Sunday not too much later, she asked her husband to carry her into the living room to watch me at a Calvary Church service on television. At the end of the program she said, "Tell Ed that I am ready to die. I prayed that prayer. I'm ready." The next day she passed away. I conducted the funeral. She was a unique individual, and as people arrived for the service, we played the Rolling Stones, Metallica, and all sorts of hard-rock bands, which had been her request. For the message, I told her story. I told about the prayer I had written out and about how she had prayed that prayer, to my surprise. It was an incredible service. I am so glad I kept going back to see her. I am so glad I persisted, even though she would not say a word to me.

Over the years, I have talked with all sorts of people who have ALS. I talk with at least one individual every week. It might not seem as fancy as preaching to five thousand people, but it is powerful. When I look into their eyes, it's as if I am looking into their souls. Even when I'm talking on the phone, it's as if they are right there in the room with me. We are both broken. We both have a limited time on earth. We both know that dying is in our future. We both know that our muscles will continue to decline. It's like we're on common ground. It's not a pastor up on the platform teaching truths to the congregation seated beneath him. It is one broken person talking to another broken person. And there is power in that.

4

PASTOR NO MORE

When I was diagnosed with ALS, I knew that my time as a pastor would be limited, but I tried not to think about it. I tried to get up every day and do the best job I could. Fortunately for me, I served another five years as pastor at Calvary Church. Doctors had originally given me two to five years to live, so being able to continue as a pastor took me to the limits of that prognosis. But I always knew that one day I would have to quit. I wondered, is there life beyond the church? Is there life beyond being a pastor? What happens if I can no longer preach? What happens if I am set aside as a counselor? What happens when there is no staff to supervise? What happens when there are no more board meetings to attend? Eventually I found out.

I had driven out the back driveway of Calvary Church several thousand times in the more than eighteen years I served there. The driveway has a steep decline and incline, like a hill. I used to love to drive fast down the hill, bottom out, and race up the other side. But this night I drove slowly. This was my last time driving away from the church. We had just finished a two-hour service, my last service as pastor. Throughout the day's services, I had said very little. In fact, I don't remember much about that Sunday at all. I left before the final service was dismissed and drove out the back driveway with my family.

Obviously I had never intended for it to end this way. I had a hard time believing that my work at Calvary Church was actually over.

As I drove away, I remembered the night I answered the call to preach. I was eighteen years old and in my second year of college. I was studying pre-med at Bob Jones University. My roommate had invited me to evangelize with him for the weekend. He asked me to bring along my soccer ball so we could get out on the street and I could juggle the ball while he shared the good news of Jesus. I didn't have to say or do anything other than juggle the ball. It was a good deal.

That Sunday night we attended church service at my roommate's small United Methodist church. I had settled in for a good nap when I heard the preacher's booming voice announce, "Jonah was called to preach, and he ran away from God." This man was the kind of preacher who yelled, sweated, and marched all over the platform. He was in his late fifties, tall, and intimidating. I couldn't help but listen intently to each word he spoke. For the next hour, I felt he preached directly to me, for I had already been struggling with whether or not I should be in ministry.

Surprisingly, throughout my early years in college, I never really asked God what I should do with my life. I assumed that my proficiency in science meant God wanted me to pursue the field, so I majored in chemistry. I wanted to enroll in medical school and eventually become a surgeon. After all, I figured a brain's a terrible thing to waste! One of the advantages of being in a Christian school is the chapel services. And one of the issues constantly raised in college chapels is "What does God want you to do with your life?" I remember after one of the chapel services where this theme was addressed, I decided to go back to my dorm room and ask God what He wanted me to do. I took out my King James Version Bible and let it open randomly.

I know, this is not the best way to seek the will of God. After all, you could follow this method and open on "Judas went and hanged himself" or "What thou doest, do quickly," which probably shouldn't be interpreted as God's plan for your life.

However, on this particular evening, my Bible opened to 1 Corinthians chapter 1. As I read along, a number of quotes spoke to me directly. "For Christ sent me not to baptize, but to preach the gospel." "For the preaching of the cross is to them that perish foolishness." "But we preach Christ crucified." It felt like God was calling me to preach. I took a deep breath and said I would keep reading and hopefully it would point me in the right direction. I read, "For ye see your calling, brethren, how that not many wise men after the flesh, not many mighty, not many noble, are called."

In truth, it was a pretty clear sign. And even though I did not surrender at that moment, I knew deep in my heart that ultimately God was calling me to preach.

So as I sat in that tiny Methodist church and listened to the passionate sermon, I felt a knowing tug in my heart. At the end of the sermon, the pastor gave a public invitation. I remember standing there toward the back, holding onto the pew in front of me. The congregation sang verse after verse of "Just As I Am," but I did not go forward. When the benediction was pronounced, I heaved a sigh of relief.

After the service, the pastor was at the back door shaking hands with people. When I got to him, I asked if we could please talk. We went down into the church basement and sat on too-small kids' chairs in a cramped Sunday school room.

After we talked for a while about what I was feeling, we both knelt down, and I said to God, "God, I think You are calling me to full-time ministry. I think You are calling me to preach. And I want You to know that tonight I surrender to You." After I returned to my room that night, I called my parents to inform them of my decision.

Now here I was, driving home after my last sermon after having been a pastor for more than eighteen years. It was over. And I really didn't know what I was going to do.

This was not the first time I had left a job I loved. I came to Calvary Church after nearly fifteen years of working with Jerry Falwell at Liberty University. After graduating from college in 1972 with my MA, I could not find a job. So I worked digging graves for my brother-in-law for six months. Then Jerry Falwell offered me a job as dean of men at what was then called Lynchburg Baptist College. When I took the job, the school was in its second year; in those days it was slightly above Sunday school status in the world of academia. There were only a few hundred students, and they were housed at the summer camp in the middle of the James River. Classes were held in the lobbies of the Thomas Road Baptist Church. But I

NOTRE DAME

After I arrived at Calvary, I was preaching one day and announced that I was a Notre Dame football fan. The crowd was so angry: all of the Michigan football fans were offended, all of the Michigan State football fans were offended, and I got all sorts of joking letters from people saying that had they known this, they never would have voted me in as pastor. At that point, I became even more of a Notre Dame football fan. Every Sunday in the fall, I would work something into the sermon about Notre Dame football.

One time while in attendance at a Notre Dame versus Michigan game (in Michigan), I noticed a blimp circling around overhead. Toward the end of the game when Notre Dame's victory was assured, I told the Michigan fans next to me that the pope was riding around in the blimp and that he was blessing all those Catholic players. They were not happy with me.

figured that working for Jerry was better than digging graves, so I took the job until I could find something better.

It took me fourteen and a half years to find something better. Over the years as I worked for Jerry, I took on a variety of responsibilities. I coached the soccer team. I taught New Testament survey. I was the vice president for student life at the university. I taught a large adult Sunday school class at Thomas Road Baptist Church. I preached every Sunday night to the university community on Liberty Mountain. I was the editor of the school magazine. I was chairman of the board of Lynchburg Christian Academy. I served on the board of the Moral Majority. I was the associate pastor at Thomas Road Baptist Church. I worked with Jerry on both television programs and radio programs, traveling the country and making appearances on everything from *Time* magazine to the *Phil Donahue Show*. And I thoroughly enjoyed everything I was doing. Jerry was one of the kindest and most compassionate men I had ever met. It was a privilege working with him and for him. I began to sense again what I had told Jerry in our first interview, that preaching and pastoring were in my blood.

In the midst of the busyness of working for Jerry Falwell, I began a one-year journey of praying and asking God if He wanted me to be a full-time pastor instead of a jack-of-all-trades. Every night, my wife and I would talk about our future and we'd pray together. We both knew we wanted to leave, but we were waiting for God to open up a door.

In the winter of 1987, I resigned from my position at Liberty University and became the senior pastor of Calvary Church in

Grand Rapids, Michigan. I felt strongly at the time that this was the leading of Jesus. He told me to get out of the boat, and I obeyed. When we left Lynchburg, we were really excited to embark on a new journey, despite having to leave all of our friends in Virginia and start over in Michigan. The thought of a whole new pilgrimage was exciting.

Over the years I had a number of opportunities to leave Calvary Church. I could have gone back into education as the president of a seminary or a university. I could have gone to another church. But every time people called with opportunities to leave, I gave them the same answer: "First, I am not interested; I believe God wants me at Calvary Church. Second, I will not pray about it, since there is nothing to pray about. I know this is where God wants me." I was not being arrogant or dismissive of the opportunities; I just knew without a doubt that I belonged at Calvary.

And now I had left it.

◆ ◆ ◆

I have a study about fifteen minutes north of Calvary Church. It's a wonderful place where I am surrounded by books. My books are scattered all over the room, but I know each one and why it is open to a certain page. Every Monday, I would go up there to start preparing my sermon for the next Sunday.

The day after I left Calvary Church, I went out to my study. Everything looked the same. My desk was cluttered with books. On the shelf next to it were all the pictures of my wife and family. I walked in and sat down at the desk. Ordinarily I would open the Bible and some books and begin studying. But that day was different. I had nothing to study for. No sermon to prepare. No passages to study. No books to pore over. Basically I had nothing to do.

So I sat all day long looking at the books, looking at my computer, and wondering what in the world I was going to do with my life now.

Being a modern man, I of course had my cell phone with me. During my days as a pastor, I often threatened to get rid of it. It rang constantly with emergency after emergency, need after need. But on that first day after my resignation, the phone never rang. It went from ringing constantly to not ringing at all. In just

PREACHING IN INDIA

For years my assistant transcribed all my sermons. One day a member of the congregation came in and asked if he could pay for a copy of each of my sermons. He was on his way to India and wanted to take several suitcases of my sermons with him. We gladly gave him copies of my teachings. Most of those copies would find their way into the hands of a pastor in India, Pastor Daniel, who used them in his own preparations to preach.

Pastor Daniel preached my sermons all over India. Eventually I found out about him, and he invited me to come to India and speak to ten thousand pastors. But my neurologist advised against the trip, so I declined the invitation. I was sad to miss the opportunity. Several people found out about Pastor Daniel's invitation and decided to bring him to Grand Rapids. We put together a television

>

one day. This was a shock to my system. In disbelief I thought, *Doesn't anyone need me?* So I picked up the landline to call my wife.

"Could you call my cell phone? I think it's broken."

She called right away. The cell phone worked.

What now? I had gone from leading a church of over five thousand people to doing nothing. And I wasn't sure what in the world I was going to do. I felt purposeless.

Fortunately I had some friends who asked me to come down to southern

> crew, and the pastor and I did fifty thirty-minute broadcasts over the next year and a half. I would speak, and then the pastor would translate in his native tongue. These programs were then used on Indian television. They were also used to help pastors all over India. One day Pastor Daniel told me, "When you get to heaven, there will be more Indians lined up to thank you than people from America." So even though I am no longer a pastor, I am, in a way, still preaching—across the world in India!

Florida and teach the Bible to a small group of people in their community. So for several winters, my wife and I flew back and forth to Florida to teach this group of people. I was so used to speaking to over five thousand people that at first it felt odd to teach a small group of thirty to forty people. But I was thankful; at least I was teaching somebody. I had a reason to use my study again, to prepare new sermons for a new group of listeners. I could keep myself somewhat busy, though nothing like the hectic days of my time as a pastor.

5

A YEAR OF LIVING LIKE JESUS

Not too long after I retired, I was driving down the road, listening to public radio. The program I was listening to was interviewing a man named A. J. Jacobs. He was agnostic and Jewish but decided that for an entire year he would write down all of the rules in the Bible and set out to obey them. He then wrote a book about it, *The Year of Living Biblically*. When I got home, I ordered his book and had it shipped overnight; I was so excited to read it. I read through it in several days. It was hilarious. I laughed my way through the entire book. Then I thought, *If this guy can do this as an agnostic, then maybe I should do something similar as a follower of Jesus.* So I decided to spend a year trying to live like Jesus.

During my year of trying to live like Jesus, I did three things. First, I tried to live as a Jew, since Jesus was Jewish. I observed the Sabbath. I went to the synagogue. I grew out my beard. I observed all the feasts and festivals. I ate kosher, as much as a Gentile could without a kosher kitchen or a wife who could cook Jewish food. At least I tried to eat the types of food in combination that Jews would eat. I also had a rabbi help me think through how Jesus would have lived. Second, I tried to *think* like Jesus. Every week, I listened to all four Gospels of Matthew, Mark, Luke, and John. There were moments while I was listening to the Gospels that I actually thought I was standing on the edge of the crowd, hearing Jesus preach. Third, I tried to obey Jesus's teachings as literally as possible.

It was an overwhelming year. A few months into it, a friend who worked at a book publisher encouraged me to consider writing a book about my experiences. I certainly didn't start the year intending to write a book, but I was learning quite a lot, and people did seem interested in hearing about it. So eventually I wrote *The Year of Living Like Jesus*. I even got the agnostic-Jewish A. J. Jacobs to write a foreword for me.

But for me, that book was not the main event. The main event was that for an entire year I was involved in something that took over my life. It gave me a sense of purpose. It gave me a sense of satisfaction. It gave me a sense that God was doing something unique in my life. It gave me a reason to live!

During that year, every day was different. I had to make choices about what to eat. No pork. No bacon. No shrimp. I had to reconsider what food was "good" for me. Every meal required a lot of planning for Lorna, who had no preparation for this year but tried not to cook food that would cause me to violate my commitment for the year. In a strict Jewish diet, milk represents life and meat represents death. So according to the laws, you cannot have both in the same meal. So every meal required lots of thought and planning. I could not eat whatever I wanted when the mood struck; I had to learn obedience and self-control.

To learn more about how Jesus thought, each day I listened to a sizable portion of the Gospels. This required lots of my time. Sometimes I would go for a walk and listen to the Scripture on my iPod. Other times I would sit at home alone and listen. Sometimes I would listen as I drove my car. But for large portions of my day, I was focused on the life and words of Jesus, and that helped me to think and act more like He did. Similar to a traditional Jewish disciple in the first century, I was trying to be just like my rabbi. And it was working.

Every day I also prayed the rosary. I know this doesn't have much to do with following Jesus in a biblical sense, but I found it useful in that it helped me focus on the entire life of Jesus—His birth, His life, His death, His resurrection, and His ascension. I also prayed the prayer rope several times a day, which is an Orthodox practice in which you repeat over and over, "Lord Jesus Christ, Son of God, have mercy on me, a sinner." These rituals took a considerable portion of my day, but they helped keep me focused on what that year was about.

I also decided that I would obey the teachings of Jesus, as naturally as possible. So every single day I was looking for ways to do that, such as praying for my enemies, loving those who oppose me, taking care of the homeless, picking up strangers, and the like. Of course the list could go on and on. It got me in trouble on several occasions, because I figured that Jesus would hang out at bars and drink beer and talk to people. I also ended up voting Democrat in the election that year, which is a capital crime for a former Moral Majority leader. But that's what I thought Jesus would have done.

My year of living like Jesus was a huge blessing for me. Every day I awoke with a unique purpose: to try to live like Jesus. Although I failed miserably in obeying all of His teachings, I certainly did try! And that effort occupied my heart, mind, and actions every day. Prior to that year, I had been obsessed with ALS. The disease and my future were constantly on my mind. But during this special year, it was much less important to me. I still thought about it, and the worry was always there, but it was no longer my primary focus.

I am so thankful for that.

6

GIVING THANKS

"Cancer has changed my life," the speaker said in a voice barely above a whisper. "It was devastating. The surgery. The chemo. The radiation. I've lost all of my hair. There were times when I could barely get off the couch, I was so weak. But I am here to tell you that for the last eighteen months, I have been cancer free."

Immediately the crowd broke into spontaneous and enthusiastic applause. After the applause died down, she continued.

"Cancer has changed my life. I don't take anything for granted anymore. I'm trying to live every moment of every day to the fullest. I appreciate my family more than I ever have. And to all of you who prayed for me: thank you. In spite of the struggle I faced with cancer, I am here to tell you that I am grateful God gave me cancer."

I have heard that statement repeated over the years:

"I am grateful God gave me cancer."

I have two problems with it. My first problem is connected to God. Does God really give people cancer? Does God give people ALS? There are plenty of theologians who would argue that God plans every detail of life. So all of the good stuff in life comes from God. And all of the bad stuff in life comes from God as well. Of course this theology is appealing when everything is going your way. But the problem comes when everything is going against you; is God really responsible then? People have said to me, "God must really trust you because He has given you this terminal disease."

Really?

I have tried to serve God faithfully all my life. Though I have not been perfect, I have tried to passionately follow Him. And now this God whom I have been following has given me this disease because He trusts me? What kind of theology is that?! I do believe God could have prevented the disease. I do believe God can still heal me. But I don't believe God is responsible for giving me this disease. We live in a broken world. It's a world of sickness, disease, and death. I believe I was genetically predisposed to ALS and that something happened in my life that triggered the disease. I don't believe God had anything to do with it. I think God will help me through it, but I don't think He is the cause.

The second problem I have with that statement concerns being grateful for the disease. Generally people who say this have been cured of their ailments. But what if God does not cure you? What if you get worse? What if you end up dying? Will you still be grateful for the disease? Honestly I have actually tried to be grateful for ALS. But with each muscle that quits working, I struggle harder to be grateful. I have tried saying to God, "I am grateful for this disease."

Even though I say the words, I really don't mean it.

Then I came across a scripture verse that helped me understand the nature of gratefulness. "In everything give thanks." It does not say "*for* everything give thanks." Rather it says "*in* everything give thanks." So I have concluded that I am not obligated to give thanks *for* the disease. Rather, I am obligated *in the midst of* the disease to be grateful for other things.

And I find there is a vast difference in being grateful *for* something and being grateful *in* something. In the midst of my struggle I can still be grateful.

After I resigned from being a pastor at Calvary Church, I was faced with a dilemma as to where Lorna and I would worship. This was a difficult challenge. For nearly two decades, I had poured my life into the congregation at Calvary Church. My friends were there. My closest colleagues were there. But it was important for me to move on. The church was in the process of selecting a new pastor, and if I continued to attend, people would ask me what I thought. So where would we go? We decided to try a large African-American church a few blocks from our home. I had known the pastor for many years and we were friends. So Lorna and I began attending the Messiah Missionary Baptist Church, and the minority population doubled. It went from two white people to four white people.

It's one thing to occasionally preach in an African-American church. It's one thing to occasionally attend the worship service at an African-American church. But to be there week after week and month after month is something entirely different. By the way, make sure you eat before you go to church. A service lasts from 10:45 a.m. to 1:15 p.m. That's two and a half hours. At Calvary Church we were able to do *two* services with a break in between in that amount of time. However, the Missionary Baptist service doesn't seem nearly that long. It is filled with music and with energy.

One of the things I noticed in this new church was the way virtually everyone prayed; it was markedly different from what I encountered at Calvary. Whether it was a deacon, a young person, or the pastor, everyone almost always began their prayers by giving thanks. "Lord, thank You for waking me up this morning. Thank You for the measure of health You have given me to be here in a house of prayer...." As odd as it is to say, I had never heard anyone begin a prayer with "Lord, thank You for waking me up this morning."

But, as I thought about it, it made a lot of sense. We are supposed to think of each day as a blessing, right? So why not give thanks for it? So now, when I wake up in the morning, I pray, "Lord, thank You for waking me up this morning." I no longer take the simple things in life for granted. I am grateful for every day God gives me. And this is where thanksgiving begins. So whatever you are facing right now, when you wake up in the morning, I challenge you to pray, "Lord, thank You for waking me up this morning."

◆ ◆ ◆

Several years before I was diagnosed with ALS, I was studying the issue of thanksgiving. I decided to do something a bit off the wall. I went into my bedroom and began thanking God for everything there.

I began with my ties, of which there were nearly fifty, most of them gifts. I thanked God individually for every tie I had. The University of Virginia ties. The Notre Dame ties. The Royal Port Rush Golf Club tie. The Royal Belfast Golf Club tie. The Liberty University tie. All of them!

Then I began thanking God for every pair of pants. I thanked God for every coat. I then went to the sweater drawer and began thanking God for every single sweater. I then went to the underwear drawer and thanked God for every single piece of underwear. I thanked God for every single T-shirt. I thanked God for every single sock, the blue ones, the black ones, the brown ones, and the Irish ones (dark blue with shamrocks!).

Then I went to the shoe closet and thanked God for each shoe. After about an hour of giving thanks for these things that seem so small and everyday, I was overwhelmed with gratitude.

REGRETS (SOCCER)

I grew up playing football (soccer) in Northern Ireland. Back in high school, I played pretty well. I had a lot of dribbling skills. I shall never forget the first game. We got to kick off. They passed back to the center midfielder, who then kicked a long ball for me, racing down the touchline. The play went well until the defender ran me over. I think he was a rugby player who missed getting on the rugby team, so he now played soccer; he was rough, tough, and big. After he hit me, I lay there on the ground. Just thirty seconds into the game and I had to leave the field. No more playing that day for me. But I learned a great lesson. Watch out for big defenders who would just as soon run you over as take the ball!

I went on to play in college and even coached at Liberty University. When I was in college, I spent at least an hour every day practicing soccer.

>

I realized how good God had been to me. And I was giving thanks only for material stuff—not the real stuff like my relationship with God through Jesus Christ. Occasionally, now, I will go through this practice of thanking God for various small things in my life. I always feel overwhelmed with gratitude when I'm done.

One of the Greek words that is translated for *thanksgiving* is *eucharisteo*. The middle part of that word is *charis*—the Greek word for *grace*. So thanksgiving then becomes my response to God's grace. However, one of the major challenges when your life falls apart is that you can lose sight of God's grace. It is very difficult to see His grace when everything seems to have gone wrong in your life. I find that giving thanks is an ongoing struggle. And there are many things for which I am not grateful! I can no longer button the buttons on my shirt. I can no longer put on a heavy jacket. I can no longer raise my right hand above my head. I can no longer write. I can no longer eat with my right hand. I eat with my left hand, and now even that is becoming a challenge. And over time all of these challenges will get worse and worse. So what in the world do I have to be grateful for?

So much.

Lord, thank You for waking me up this morning.

Lord, thank You that I can still turn over in bed.

Lord, thank You that I can still get out of bed.

Lord, thank You that I can walk to the bathroom.

> Eventually I surrendered to the Lord, and I knew that it was either the word of the Lord or soccer. So I promised the Lord that for every hour I would practice soccer, I would also read the Bible for an equal amount of time.

Actually my time devoted to soccer was greatly reduced!

But I do have one regret. Could I have played professional soccer? The truth is, I don't know. But when I was at Liberty University, one of the coaches who had played in the English first division told me that I could likely play in the first division in England. "If we had gotten you as an eighteen-year-old, and if you could put on some weight, you could probably play professional soccer." So I have often wondered to this day what my life would have been like if I had stayed in Ireland and ended up playing professional soccer. But I don't think too long about it. After all, I am really grateful for the privilege of teaching and preaching God's Word. That's a whole lot better than playing soccer.

Lord, thank You that I can still go to the bathroom by myself.

Lord, thank You that I can still brush my teeth.

Lord, thank You that I can still take a shower.

Lord, thank You that I can still use a towel to dry myself off.

Lord, thank You that I can still eat breakfast.

Lord, thank You that I can still dress myself.

Lord, thank You that I can still drive my car.

Lord, thank You that I can still walk.

Lord, thank You that I can still talk.

And the list goes on and on and on. I have learned in my journey with ALS to focus on what I can do, not on what I can't do. I have learned to be grateful for the small things in life and for the many things I can still do. Of course, once in a while I grieve what I can no longer do. But I don't let those periods of grief go on too long. I keep coming back to what I can do. And I am grateful that God in His grace has allowed me to do so many things.

7

WHEN GOD IS SILENT

Over the past eleven years, several thousands of people have prayed for my healing. Many of these are people who are serious about their faith. These are people who believe in the healing power of God. These are people who believe in the promises of the Bible, including promises for healing. But so far none of their prayers have worked. My condition gets worse and worse. I can do less today than I could a year ago. So what about all the prayers? Has God ignored them? Does He even listen? Is it worth praying?

Recently two people came to see me. They wanted to know if I had ever been prayed over for healing.

"I really believe that God wants to heal you," one of them said. "Would you mind if we prayed for you? We believe that God wants to heal you."

"Of course I would like for you to pray that God would heal me," I said. But I was really thinking that their prayers would be a waste of time. Many others were praying for my healing, and so far none of the prayers worked. But maybe these two people were different. Maybe their prayers would work.

One of the men took my hand and the other placed his hands on my shoulder. As they prayed, the one kept squeezing my hand tighter and tighter, while the other kept pressing harder and harder on my shoulders. I thought for a moment they must have believed God would only hear the prayers of people who squeezed and pressed harder than the rest!

They prayed, "Lord Jesus, You are the One who can ultimately heal us. We plead Your blood over the life of Ed Dobson. You are the One who heals. And by faith, we claim Your immediate healing for Ed Dobson."

The pair continued for some time, although I don't remember all that was said. But I do remember that at the end, the one who was praying asked me, "Did you feel anything?"

"No."

"Well, when I prayed, I believed that God would immediately heal you. So I asked you if you felt anything."

"No, I didn't feel a thing."

The two men immediately got up and left. No words of encouragement. No explanation for their prayers. I figured they had done their thing and prayed for healing. Maybe it was my lack of faith to blame. Maybe it was my cynical attitude. Maybe it was because I knew that no one had ever been healed of ALS. Whatever the reason, they left.

I've had similar experiences multiple times over the years, sometimes in churches after I've preached, sometimes in a coffee shop. Always it was with people who believed that when they prayed, God would answer them right away. Maybe they had success with this in other situations and consequently thought God would intervene every time. But God did not answer their prayers for me. So has God abandoned me?

Have you ever prayed for something that was reasonable and necessary but God ignored you? Have you ever felt abandoned by God? Of course you have; we all have! Some theologians say that when God answers a prayer, He does so in one of three ways: He answers it either "yes," "no," or "wait." So in my situation of praying for healing from ALS, God has answered my prayer with either "no" or "wait." And I find this answer rather unsatisfying! If God has the power to heal, and if God really loves me, then why in the world is He not healing me?

So where do I find God when heaven is silent?

Over the years, I have found Him in the family and friends He has put around me. They have become the hands of God. They have become the face of God. They have become the feet of God. They have become the heart of God in my life.

In no one do I see the love of God as I see it in my wife. Lorna has always kept life in perspective for me and knows just what to say to get my head in the right place.

About two months after I was diagnosed, we were sitting in a coffeehouse, drinking cappuccino from two very large mugs. In the middle of our conversation, I said, "Look, I can still lift my cup to my mouth."

Lorna replied, "Why is it every time we talk, you always bring up the disease? Don't you think there's more to life than ALS?"

She was right. Every time we talked, I brought it up. Lorna made me realize that my life and future could not be measured by the disease.

I am now more than eleven years into the disease, and I could not exist without the help of my wife. She helps me dress. She makes my protein drink each morning. She cuts my food. She puts on my ski cap and helps me into my winter coat. She ties my shoes. And the list goes on and on. I am deeply grateful for her. When we married forty years ago, we repeated vows to each other, which included "in sickness and in health." When I made that vow, I never dreamed I would need this much help. ALS is not something we ever planned on, but it is the reality that we face.

Fortunately I have a slow-growing form of the disease, so I have time to adjust when my muscles quit working. Eventually I found that it was taking me longer and longer to button up my shirts. When Lorna offered to help me, I quickly refused, the stubborn Irishman I am. But as the disease progressed, it was taking me at least five minutes to button my shirts, and by the time I finished, I was tired. And I was frequently quite angry with my fingers for not cooperating.

At one of my visits at the University of Michigan ALS clinic, my wife mentioned the difficulty I was having with my buttons. "You have a choice to make," the head of the clinic said. "You can waste all your energy buttoning your shirts and have little energy for the rest of the day. Or you can ask for help and save your energy for the things that really matter—like your family."

I really didn't want to hear her advice, but it stuck with me and I thought about it during the ride home. So the next morning I asked my wife to help me button my shirts. Eventually it became too difficult for me to button my shirts, even with her help. At some point, a friend suggested she put Velcro on my shirts, which she did. And now, my shirts look like they are buttoned up. I call them my "Superman shirts," because now I can rip them off at any time. Actually, it takes me quite a while to rip them off.

Thinking about my stubborn past with my buttons makes me wonder, why do I have such a difficult time asking for help? I'm not sure. Maybe it is because I spent so much of my life helping others in pastoral ministry: going to the hospital in the middle of the night, meeting the family at the funeral home, praying for someone in the office. It seems like my life was filled with crisis after crisis. But I enjoyed every minute of it, because I felt useful and like I was making a difference. But now I'm at a point where it is I who need help, yet it is very difficult to ask. Or maybe I have a hard time asking for help because I'm a man. Men like to be in charge, to be in control. We like doing things our own way. But now I am no longer in charge or in control. Now I can no longer do it my way. I desperately need the help of others, and I'm thankful that I can admit it.

It was the middle of my last Sunday at Calvary Church. I was overwhelmed with sorrow and grief. This was the one job I really loved, and now I could no longer do it. People were constantly asking me, "How do you feel about leaving the church?" I was tired of this question. I felt terrible about leaving. But I would smile and respond, "I really have no other choice. This is what God wants at this point in my life. I will really miss all the people in the church."

For the service, I decided we would do Communion, which typically takes the entire time and is our only focus. During the service, I would give a brief five-minute meditation to help us focus on Communion. On this last Sunday, though, I asked someone else to do the meditation. I wanted the church to know that it was not about me—it was about Jesus and what He had done on the cross.

Toward the end of the second service that day, I was overcome with emotion. I could not believe this was my last Sunday. As I served Communion to the elders and looked into their faces, I started to cry. So I asked the associate pastor to finish the service, and I slipped out early. I walked down the back stairs and along the hallway to my office. I just wanted to be alone. I wanted to have a good cry and then be prepared for the third service. As I passed the entrance that leads to the parking lot, a couple was coming through the doors.

"Could I have a word with you?" the man asked.

I really didn't want to have a word with anybody, but I was still being paid to be the pastor and, therefore, paid to be nice.

"Sure," I answered. I was afraid this man wanted to know how I was doing and would ask me the same questions I had grown tired of hearing.

We walked down the hall and into my office.

"I am J. J. Bouma, and this is my wife, Pam. We have been coming to Calvary Church for twelve years, but we have never met you. We never come to the second service, and we never come to this door by the offices. On the way to church this morning, my wife and I were praying that somehow we would bump into you. You see, on Friday I was diagnosed with ALS."

At that moment I was overwhelmed. Here I was, totally consumed with leaving the church. But now I was faced with a man who had just been diagnosed with ALS and who had prayed that he would bump into me here this morning. For me, this meeting was a reminder that God is still involved in the details of my life and of this man's. I made arrangements with the man to meet him and his wife for coffee.

We met later that week for coffee and had a long talk. I asked him a series of questions about his disease. When did you first notice symptoms? Where were you diagnosed? Have you sought a second opinion?

In the course of the conversation, he told me that he had always wanted to go to Israel. I told him that I was going in the fall and that he and his wife were welcome to go with me. J. J. also told me he had just bought a brand-new red Corvette. He planned to drive across the country on Route 66, from Chicago to California. J. J. and Pam had a small group of friends who did something unique together every month. When the friends heard about his plan to travel Route 66, they all agreed to buy Corvettes and join him. He invited me and Lorna to go along and be a part of the trip.

J. J. and Pam went to Israel with us, but the eleven-hour flight over to Israel wore J. J. out. He wasn't even sure if he could go to any of the sites. But he did it anyway. We were eating lunch together in the picnic area at one of the sites, and I had to go to the bathroom. When I walked in, J. J. was in there, and he was gasping for breath. I walked up next to him and said, "This is a nasty disease."

He said one word: "Yep."

I don't remember much else on the trip, but I clearly and distinctly remember that moment.

By the time the Corvette trip was to begin, J. J. and I had grown quite close, and I decided to participate with the group. This trip was an unbelievable experience. Our party included fourteen Corvettes, a recreational vehicle, and a bus. We decided to use the trip to raise money for ALS research as well as to visit people with ALS all across the country. By the time we set off, it was difficult to understand J. J. when he spoke, and I became his designated spokesperson. For me, the highlight of the trip was in Oklahoma. We arranged a visit to the Oklahoma State Police training ground, where officers are trained to drive their cars. We sat through about an hour of instruction before taking our Corvettes for a race around the track. It was unbelievably fun. Not surprisingly, our skilled instructor drove faster in his car than any of us could in the Corvettes—and he was driving in reverse!

Not only was the trip fun in and of itself, but it was also a wonderful blessing to J. J. and, frankly, to me. Touring the country to bring awareness about ALS, meeting others afflicted with the disease, and seeing the immense support of J. J.'s friends were things I will never forget. We saw God every day on that trip: in the people we met, in the laughs and fears we shared, and in the comfort of knowing we were not alone.

I spent a lot of time with J. J. Toward the end, in late fall, I met him down in Florida for a visit. By this time, he had a feeding tube and was riding a scooter to get around. We went for a walk together, me walking and him on the scooter. J. J. told me that he did not think he would make it to Christmas. I was so sad to hear this. And much sadder when he was right. I was at the house when he passed away. After he had gone, Pam took me into a separate room and showed me a legal document.

"J. J. wanted you to have this."

I read the document, which said he had willed me his Corvette. At first I declined it, but Pam told me that I had no choice but to take it. I wondered what his children would say, so I declined it again. "This is what J. J. wanted to do for you, so you have no other choice but to take it."

I just recently gave the Corvette back because I can't drive it anymore, but for a while there, if you saw me driving around in a red Corvette, it wasn't really mine. It was J. J. Bouma's, and he is not here because he is in heaven.

When Jesus was on the cross, He prayed, "My God, my God, why have you forsaken me?" (Matthew 27:46). Theologians suggest that while Jesus was on the cross, He took the sins of the whole world on Himself. And God, who is holy, cannot stand to look on sin. Consequently He turned His back on His only Son. That may be true.

I think that when Jesus was on the cross, He experienced the fullness of His own humanity. In the fullness of that humanity, He felt abandoned by God. Whether or not God actually turned His back on Jesus, I don't know. What I do know is that Jesus felt forsaken by God. I find great encouragement in the idea that the Son felt abandoned. First, this means it's okay to question God. I like the idea that Jesus questioned His own father and, in so doing, gave me permission to question the Father as well. Second, the life of Jesus must not and cannot be judged by this statement on the cross. We all lose sight of God for a moment here or there. We may even lose sight of God for a while. But He will show up. Three days later, Jesus was raised from the dead. Forty days later, He ascended to the right hand of God the Father. I know where J. J. is. He is in a much better place. He is free of ALS. Of course I still miss him desperately. But I know one day I will join him.

8

FORGIVENESS

"This is to be a lasting ordinance for you: On the tenth day of the seventh month you must deny yourselves and not do any work—whether native-born or a foreigner residing among you—because on this day atonement will be made for you, to cleanse you. Then, before the LORD, you will be clean from all your sins. It is a day of sabbath of rest, and you must deny yourselves; it is a lasting ordinance" (Leviticus 16:29–31).

This is the concluding section in the Torah and deals with the day of atonement, Yom Kippur. This is the most important day in the Jewish calendar. On this day, God forgave all the sins of the entire community—not just individual sins, not just family sins, but rather the sins of the entire Israelite community. During the celebration at the temple, the high priest would take two goats.

One goat was killed and the blood sprinkled before the ark of the covenant in the Holy of Holies. The high priest would then take the other goat, confess the sins of the entire community on its head, and then a person would lead the goat out into the wilderness and push it off a cliff.

In this closing section of the instructions for the day of atonement, it states, "Then, before the LORD, you will be clean from all your sins." There are actually two ways to interpret this verse. First, since all sins are committed before the Lord, then all sins will be forgiven. This would include sins against God and sins against others. Second, only sins "before the LORD" will be forgiven. Many rabbis interpret this statement to mean only offenses that have been committed against God will be forgiven. For all offenses committed against another person, you must go to that person and seek his or her forgiveness.

My oldest son studied in Israel for almost three years, and several of the classes were taught by rabbis. During one of the classes, the rabbi said, "I know there are several Christians in this class. If I have said anything that has been offensive to you, please forgive me." After class, my son went up to the rabbi. "Why did you ask us Christians for forgiveness?" The rabbi responded, "It's almost time for Yom Kippur, so I am going to everyone I know and asking their forgiveness for things that I have said that might have offended them."

Jesus picked up on this idea of forgiveness in the Gospels. However, He took it one step further: "For if you forgive other people when they sin against you, your heavenly Father will also forgive you. But if you do not forgive others their sins, your Father will not forgive your sins" (Matthew 6:14–15). That's a whole other level of forgiveness. Jesus argued that unless we are willing to forgive others, God will not forgive us.

In the book of Acts, Paul was brought to trial before the governor named Felix. In his defense, Paul stated, "So I strive always to keep my conscience clear before God and man" (Acts 24:16). Paul had come to grips with the instructions given to the day of atonement. Paul had taken his teachings of Jesus seriously. He wanted to live his life in such a way that he did not offend God or anyone else. And he continually strove to meet that goal.

As I look back on my years of ministry, there are a number of people I know I have offended. Since I am going to die, I want to at least ask their forgiveness. I want to be able to say with Paul, "I am striving to keep my conscience clear before God and man." So I made a list of the people I know I have offended. Because of my history with Bob Jones University, Liberty University, and the Moral Majority, that list included Bob Jones III, Jerry Falwell, and James Dobson.

First up, Bob Jones University.

After I graduated high school, my dad decided that I should go to a Christian college until I turned eighteen, and then I could go wherever I wanted. The only Christian college my dad had ever heard of was Bob Jones University, so he drove me down to the school to drop me off. I shall never forget his last words: "Now, son, don't you believe a word they tell you here unless you can prove it from the Bible!" In other words, question everything.

Bob Jones University is a very fundamentalist school. The dress code for guys is strict: a shirt and tie. Hair must be short. It cannot touch the ear or the back of the collar. The dress code for girls is also strict: girls wear dresses to class. And the dress must come down to the middle of the knee. I won't bore you with all the rules, or at least the rules as they were when I attended the school. I earned both a bachelor's degree and a master's degree at Bob Jones University. In fact, all of my formal training for ministry came from that school.

But during my last year of graduate studies, I got into some trouble. Actually, it was serious trouble. So serious that the administration voted on whether or not to graduate me.

One day Bob Jones III was preaching in chapel. He was preaching about compromise. He was imploring us never to compromise. At the end of the sermon, he asked everyone to stand who promised never to compromise. So I stood along with thousands of others. Bob Jones then went on to explain what he meant by compromise, and it sounded to me that compromise meant disagreeing with Bob Jones University.

So I sat back down.

I remembered the words of my dad: "Don't you believe a word they tell you here unless you can prove it from the Bible!" I was really committed to not compromising my belief in the Bible. And I was not committed to agreeing with Bob Jones University on everything they stood for.

The next day I got a notice to see the director of ministerial services. I went to see him, and he was very upset with me. "You are a leader here on campus. Everyone is watching you. And so when you sat down, you set a bad example." The meeting did not go well. So a few days later I was asked to meet with Bob Jones III and Bob Jones Jr. I met them after chapel.

"We are very upset with you. You are a leader here on campus and for you to sit down sets a terrible example." I'd heard this before.

"I thought that in the invitation it was between you and God. Not you and Bob Jones University," I said.

This made Bob Jones Jr. all the more angry.

"You are just like Billy Graham," he said. "He took advantage of all of the blessings of Bob Jones University and then turned his back on everything we stood for."

I was thinking, I have never been associated with Billy Graham before. For me, that's pretty good company. If I can make as big an impact as he has, I will be very successful. Of course I didn't say that to the Joneses.

I don't remember all the details of what was said back-and-forth, but they were clearly furious with me. They claimed that I was ungrateful. They claimed I was headed in the wrong direction. They claimed I was no better than Billy Graham.

But that was not the end of all my troubles. During graduate school I traveled with a small singing group, and we preached all over the South. One Sunday we were invited to Jerry Falwell's church to sing at an outreach for high school students. We sang and I preached. The trio was asked to sing at the main service, which was then televised all over the country. We were sitting together in the green room right before the church service.

"We have a problem," I said.

"What's the problem?" one of our group said.

"We were supposed to have every song checked by the music department. If you don't have your songs approved, then you are not supposed to sing them. And none of our songs have been checked by the music department."

So we quickly made a decision. We asked Jerry Falwell not to mention Bob Jones University when he introduced us to sing.

"We have a group with us to sing today from an up-and-coming school in South Carolina," Jerry Falwell said. Of course everyone knew where we were from. Several weeks later the program was on in Greenville, South Carolina—home of Bob Jones University. One of the administrators saw the program and really objected to the fact that Jerry Falwell did not give Bob Jones University credit. We got in serious trouble. And since I was the one who had made the decision not to mention Bob Jones University, I got in the most trouble.

I was called in to administration, and they lectured me about being proud of the school. I was proud of the school! I was just afraid that the songs hadn't been approved. They didn't see it the same way.

Because of all this, they held a vote to decide whether or not I would be allowed to graduate. I passed!

Several years after I received my master's degree from Bob Jones University, I was working for Jerry Falwell in Lynchburg, Virginia. One day I got a letter from one of the university's deans. Apparently he had listened to a recent sermon of mine in which I was "making fun" of Bob Jones University. He went on to inform me that I was "ungrateful" for my time at the university. As a result of that one sermon, I was banned from the campus. Of course I knew what that meant. It meant that if I went on the campus, the police would escort me off campus.

I took the letter as a badge of honor. I had been officially excommunicated from Bob Jones University. Whenever someone would find out that I attended the university, I would quickly add, "but I am no longer welcome on the campus. I have been excommunicated."

Over the years I have had mixed feelings about Bob Jones University. On one hand, I appreciate all the education that I received there. It was first-class. I met my wife there. But on the other hand, I'm glad that I am no longer associated with the school. On several occasions over the years, I talked with Bob Jones III. I felt these were important conversations. So when I made a list of the people I had offended, he was the first one to come to mind. So I called him.

"Dr. Bob, this is Ed Dobson. Recently I was diagnosed with ALS. I know that over the years I have offended you and Bob Jones University. I want you to know that I am sorry, and I am asking you to forgive me."

That was all I said. I didn't go into details about what they had done wrong and what I had done wrong. I simply acknowledged that I was wrong and asked his forgiveness. There was a long silence on the phone.

"Thank you. I want you to know that I have a Christian obligation to forgive you."

A Christian obligation? Could he not have found other language than this? I was slightly offended by his response, but the more I've thought about it, the more I realize it was a biblical response. Again my dad's words came back to me. Bob Jones was just quoting the Bible. I was doing my Christian obligation: I wanted to clear my conscience with everyone I had offended. Bob Jones was doing his Christian obligation: he was forgiving me.

◆ ◆ ◆

When I arrived in Grand Rapids in 1987, I decided that I wanted to figure out what it meant to be a pastor in the local community. So I declined all media opportunities that came up because of my former work with Jerry Falwell and the Moral Majority. I realized that the church was filled primarily with Republicans but also quite a few Democrats. So I decided early on that we would be nonpolitical. Of course this did not mean that I would never preach on moral issues. As I worked my way through the Bible, I often came across moral issues, and I was never hesitant to preach on them. But we would be nonpartisan and nonpolitical. No voter guides. No registration to vote. No reminders of voting. We simply wanted to be a church.

A number of years ago my good friend Cal Thomas and I wrote a book titled *Blinded by Might: Why the Religious Right Can't Save America*. Our intent was to call the church back to being the church. To win people back family by family, house by house, street by street and to transform the culture from the bottom up. We reflected on our days with the Moral Majority and the religious Right. And our reflections were at times critical of what went on. Jerry Falwell was not happy! We gave him an advance copy of the book, and during a telephone conversation with him, he suggested a number of changes. Cal and I agreed to those changes. But he was still not happy.

PHIL DONAHUE

I thoroughly enjoyed every part of my ministry with Jerry Falwell and Liberty University.

On one occasion, I flew to New York City to debate on the *Phil Donahue Show*. The show's guests for the day were a Boy Scout and his mom, both of whom were atheists. The boy had been thrown out of the Boy Scouts because he wouldn't pledge allegiance to God. When I was introduced as working for Jerry Falwell, the crowd booed.

Though I liked the kid and his mom, my position was that the Boy Scouts were justified: as a private organization, they had the right to demand allegiance to God. I remember saying in the middle of the show that it would be like joining a vegetarian organization and demanding they eat meat.

On my way back to Lynchburg, I was at the Charlotte airport. One of the Bible teachers from Liberty University was there as well. We got into a conversation.

"Where have you been?" he asked.

"I've been on the *Phil Donahue Show*."

So I decided to call Jerry Falwell after my ALS diagnosis and apologize.

"Jerry, this is Ed. I'm calling to apologize for all the times that I offended you in what I said or did."

I had barely gotten the words out of my mouth when he responded.

"Ed, you have never offended me. But you're asking for forgiveness, so I give it to you."

Never offended him? Was he kidding? Actually, he wasn't kidding. Jerry had the remarkable ability of not holding grudges against someone. Even his most bitter enemies often became his friends. Shortly after my apology, he invited me down to his church to preach on a Sunday night. I preached on the lessons I had been learning through ALS, one of which was the issue of forgiveness, and I publicly apologized to him again.

♦ ♦ ♦

I had never met James Dobson. Of course, like many others, I listened to him on the radio whenever I could. He was so helpful in how to raise children. I loved his radio show. He has done more to help families in this country than any other single person. At that distance, I loved him. But after the book *Blinded by Might* came out, James Dobson was critical of Cal and me for several days on his radio program.

I actually don't remember specifically what he said, but he was harsh and critical of us. It was weird to be

> "You're wasting your time on the *Phil Donahue Show.*"
>
> "I've been representing biblical ethics in a forum where nearly everyone is against it."
>
> "You're casting your pearls before swine."
>
> "What do you mean?"
>
> "You have been called to be a pastor and a preacher, and anything you do that takes away from that is the equivalent of casting your pearls before swine."
>
> Of course I completely disagreed with him, but I could not escape the conversation.
>
> When I landed in Lynchburg, my wife picked me up. I was telling her about the drama of the *Phil Donahue Show*. I told her blow by blow about the limousine that picked me up, meeting Phil, and of course the high drama of one hour on his show. She listened attentively, and when we pulled in the driveway, she said, "That's nice. But the garbage needs taken up to the dump."
>
> As I got into my pickup to take the garbage to the dump, I realized that real ministry does not occur in the lights of television but rather in taking garbage to the dump.

driving down the road listening to *Focus on the Family* and hearing James Dobson criticize me. There were several people in our church who were financial supporters of Focus on the Family. One of them called James Dobson and told him that he needed to meet with me. So I flew down with a good friend and we spent the day discussing the various issues in our book. We ended up agreeing to disagree. I did not convince him one iota, and he did not convince me one iota.

So when I made my list, James Dobson was on it. But before I could call him, he called me.

"I just heard about your diagnosis of ALS. I wanted you to know that Shirley and I prayed for you this morning. And we believe in divine healing."

"Thank you for calling. Actually you were on my list to call. I know that I have offended you in what I have written and said, so I want to apologize to you."

"Thank you. And you are forgiven. But I know that I have offended you in what I said, and I'm asking your forgiveness as well."

He beat me to the punch. I never expected James Dobson to call me, and I never expected him to apologize for what he had done. Those few moments on the phone were incredibly liberating for me.

I have to admit that when I was thinking about calling Bob Jones, Jerry Falwell, and James Dobson, I was nervous. These are powerful men with no need to take my phone call. I thought that they would assume that they were right and I was wrong. And I knew deep inside that I was more right than they were. But finally I decided that my relationship is more important than who's wrong and who's right. And I am really glad I made the calls, especially since Jerry Falwell is no longer with us. I am so glad I apologized to him while I could.

◆ ◆ ◆

It's one thing to ask forgiveness when you think you're right. But it's something entirely different when you know you're wrong.

One of the things I did was to make a list of every staff member we had let go at Calvary Church. I prayed over the list and settled on several people whom I knew the church had done wrong. One of them was Kathy, who had been a counselor for a number of years at the church. I was aware that there were some elders who were concerned about her style of counseling. However, I frequently referred people to her and she did a wonderful job.

Eventually, though, the elders decided that she should move on. I actually had nothing to do with the final decision, but as the pastor, I felt a responsibility for how it had all come about. She had really struggled with the church's decision. She felt abandoned. She felt betrayed. She had even come to me right after she was dismissed, and I ended up leaving before the interview was over. I knew she should be on my list.

I called her up and asked if I could see her. At that time she was working as a counselor at Mars Hill Bible Church. She agreed, so I took another pastor with me and went to see her. I walked in, got down on my knees, and asked her to forgive me. Looking someone in the eyes is much harder than talking on the telephone. It's much harder than writing an email. It's much harder than leaving a voicemail. It's looking into the person's soul, and when she looked into my eyes, she knew I was genuinely sorry.

I found out much later that this was an event that had marked her for the rest of her life. I didn't do it to mark her for the rest of her life; I did it because it was the right thing to do. I did it so that I could live my life without regret.

What if once a year in every church, everybody apologized to each other for the wrongs they had done? That would be incredible. That would be revolutionary. That would be very Jesus-like! I don't think it would be that impractical. You could go to everyone you have a relationship with and ask that person for forgiveness. It might take an entire Sunday morning service, but wouldn't it be worth it?

And then, of course, we must forgive as we have been forgiven. I think of Pope John Paul, who met with the man who tried to assassinate him and forgave him. I think of the Mennonite families who forgave the man who entered their community's schoolhouse and killed their children. Part of the Lord's Prayer is that we ask God to forgive us as we have forgiven others.

We ask for forgiveness. And we forgive others who ask us. In that way, we can experience healing, healing in our souls.

9

WORRY

"Therefore do not worry about tomorrow, for tomorrow will worry about itself. Each day has enough trouble of its own" (Matthew 6:34).

This is a statement from Jesus's Sermon on the Mount. I like it when He says "each day has enough trouble of its own." However, I get uncomfortable when He says "do not worry about tomorrow." For me, tomorrow brings great uncertainty. How can I not worry about it? My tomorrows are filled with increasing disability. My tomorrows are filled with the possibility of feeding tubes, breathing assistance, and wheelchairs.

The Internet is both a blessing and a curse. It is a blessing because it has so much information about ALS. It is a curse because that information is very depressing and serves to increase my worry about the future. I know some people with ALS who do not read any of the information the doctors give them or research the disease online. They would prefer not to know what the future holds. Sometimes I envy these people. Even though they are somewhat ignorant of the path ahead, they are perhaps better able to enjoy the present moment, as their thoughts aren't as occupied with worry as mine.

To "write" this book, I used a voice-activated computer program, since I can type only a few words at a time before my fingers wear out. Years ago I quit using my right hand to feed myself. Even though I am right-handed, if I tried to lift food to my mouth with my right hand, it would be all over the place. So I have been using my left hand for years. But now my left hand is beginning to weaken; I have to rest between bites. So I wonder, what will I do when neither hand works? ALS is a disease that constantly requires adjustment. Just about the time you become accustomed to one muscle not working, another one fails. And there is nothing you can do about it; you just have to constantly adjust how you live. So when Jesus says "do not worry about tomorrow," I find that incredibly difficult to do. It's easy to teach about not worrying about tomorrow. It is incredibly hard to live it. In fact, it's nearly impossible not to worry about tomorrow.

◆ ◆ ◆

It was the first spring after my diagnosis. I had made it through Thanksgiving. I had made it through Christmas. And now I was standing on my porch looking out the window. The leaves were coming out on the trees. Some of the bushes and flowers were beginning to blossom. The grass was coming alive. It had been a long, hard winter, but spring was finally here. No more snow. No more cloudy days. No more freezing temperatures. No more scraping the windshield on the car. All of that had passed. It was a new season, and I was beginning to think death might not be around the next corner.

As I stood there looking out the window, I noticed a bird sitting atop a bush near the house, its head constantly moving. It looked this way and that way. Then after a short period of time, it flew away. As I stood there watching it, I began thinking. *I wish I was a bird and not a man. I wish I could fly away like that bird. I would fly away from all my troubles and my disease.*

Then I remembered the words of the psalmist.

> My heart is in anguish within me;
> the terrors of death have fallen on me.
> Fear and trembling have beset me;
> horror has overwhelmed me.
> I said, "Oh, that I had the wings of a dove!
> I would fly away and be at rest.
> I would flee far away
> and stay in the desert;

> I would hurry to my place of shelter,
>   far from the tempest and storm. (Psalm 55:4–8)

That was exactly how I felt. I felt all around me the terrors of death. I wished it would all go away. I wished I could fly away and escape what the future holds for me. Unfortunately, I could not. I cannot.

So how have I coped with worry and uncertainty over the past decade? It hasn't been possible for me to completely stop worrying about tomorrow. But I have discovered a way to focus on the present moment and not be discouraged by what may come. Many months after my diagnosis, I came across some verses that continually help me focus on today.

> God has said, "Never will I leave you; never will
> I forsake you."
>   So we say with confidence, "The Lord is my
> helper; I will not be afraid. What can mere mor-
> tals do to me?" (Hebrews 13:5–6)

I wrote out these verses on several index cards. I put one next to the bed. I put another on the bathroom mirror. I put one in my office. I put another in my car. Whenever I would begin thinking about the future and start sinking into the fog, I would take a five-minute time-out. I would look at the card and repeat the verses for five minutes. The first time I quoted them, I barely believed a single word. But as I repeated them, they began to sink into my mind and soul. By the time I had finished, I was refocused on the present and not distracted by the future.

During his first year of college, my youngest son, Daniel, decided to join the Army National Guard. He had always been a patriotic person, and he wanted to serve his country. The following fall, he found out he could volunteer as a replacement soldier for a unit already in Iraq. It was a transportation unit, which had been his area of expertise during training the previous summer. So he volunteered to go to war.

Lorna and I drove Daniel an hour and a half to drop him off at the armory. The three of us hardly spoke during the trip. There was both so much and so little to be said. It was the worst drive I have ever experienced. We were sending our youngest son off to war. It was surreal. Saying good-bye was far worse than dealing with ALS. While ALS was certainly teaching me about not being in control, letting Daniel go took not being in control to a completely new level. Saying good-bye was the worst moment of my life.

As we parted, I handed my son the first card I had ever written with the verses from Hebrews: "God has said, 'Never will I leave you; never will I forsake you.' So we say with confidence, 'The Lord is my helper; I will not be afraid.'" I wanted Daniel to have the verses that had brought me such comfort. I wanted him to know that God was with him, wherever the Army took him.

It wasn't until years after Daniel's return home that I learned that card had touched many lives. Daniel put it on the dash of every truck he rode in. On one occasion, his friend was in the gun truck, and it was hit by an IED. His friend was medevaced to the hospital. That night Daniel went to visit him, and he gave the card to his friend. The kid recovered, and every time he got into the truck, he put that same card on inside of the windshield.

10

HEALING

A few months after I was diagnosed with ALS, I led a trip to Israel. On the long flight over, I did not sleep well. I kept thinking about whether or not I would be able to walk to the various sites. And if I could not walk, what would I do? I worried about speaking all day. Would my voice give out? What would I do if it did? I was so full of worry and doubt about myself; I thought I was much weaker than I was. Happily, the trip went well; I was able to walk everywhere, and my voice was as good at the end of the day as it was at the beginning.

During our visit, I was looking forward to being at the Western Wall. The Western Wall is actually the retaining wall on top of which the Temple Mount was built. When you pray there, you take a piece of paper, write out your requests, and insert it into the cracks of the wall. Over the years, millions of requests have been left in the wall. None of them are thrown away. So I wanted to write out a prayer for healing, go to the wall, put my hand on it, and pray. Finally the day came when we visited the wall.

Men and women do not pray together at the Western Wall. There is a large section where the men pray and a much smaller section where the women pray. That day, there were probably around fifty people gathered at the wall for prayer. I found a spot on the wall and carefully placed my prayer for healing in one of its cracks. I put my hand on the wall and began to pray. I was standing next to an Orthodox Jew. He was dressed in black, was wearing a hat, and had a long white beard. He was holding a prayer book and swayed back and forth as he muttered words in Hebrew. I felt strange standing next to this man, as I was dressed in a T-shirt, hiking pants, hiking boots, and a hat. Of course he never even acknowledged that I was standing next to him, as he was focused on his prayer. But I like to think that man and I shared something special together.

Next to the Western Wall is a dark tunnel leading to a number of synagogues. As I walked through the tunnel, another Orthodox Jew spoke to me.

"Are you Jewish?" he asked.

"No, I am not."

"What are you doing here?"

"I was recently diagnosed with ALS, which is a terminal disease. So I came to the Western Wall to pray for healing."

"Would you like me to pray for you?"

"Yes, please."

So he began the official Hebrew prayer for healing. I was able to pick out a few words here and there, but for the most part, I did not understand what he was saying. But I had this incredible feeling inside that God would actually listen to the prayers of this Orthodox Jew. *Maybe this is it*, I thought. *Maybe this is the way God will heal me.*

When the man had finished the prayer, I was pretty overcome with emotion.

"Thank you very, very much," I said.

"You are welcome. We are in the process of building a new synagogue, and I was wondering if you could give me $25 to help with the building."

My hopeful feelings for healing began to fade. I reluctantly reached into my pocket and gave him $25. As I gave him the money, another man walked up and joined in the conversation.

"This is my assistant," the first man said. "Could you give him $25 as well?"

At this point I had lost all of my good feelings and was mad. I felt my suffering had been exploited. But I reached into my pocket and took out another $25 anyway. My fury increased as I exited the tunnel. I had just lost $50. When I rejoined the group, I told my wife about wasting the money. My voice rose, and my arms flailed as I recounted what happened.

Lorna listened carefully to what I said. After I finished, she looked at me with her wise, kind eyes and asked, "But what if his prayer works?"

"God will heal you if you have enough faith."

I have always believed in God's power to heal. And I believe He can heal anything, including ALS. However, it is not always the will of God to heal. I am happy to say that I have prayed for people who have been miraculously cured of their ailments. But most of the people I have prayed for were not healed. So while I have always believed in the power of God to heal, I also believe that healing is ultimately up to God and God alone; it is not up to us.

There are some theologians who believe that it is the will of God to always heal. After all, the prophet Isaiah stated, "By his wounds we are healed." Also, often in the Gospels when Jesus wanted to heal someone, He asked them, "Do you believe that I am able to do this?" When the person responded affirmatively, Jesus healed them. Therefore, some theologians argue that ultimately healing is up to us, and if we have enough faith, we will indeed be healed. To these theologians, faith is the complete absence of doubt. So if you doubt at all, you do not have true faith and will not be healed.

Of course I would like to have that kind of doubtless faith. I would like to be able to trust God without any doubts at all. But is healing really conditional upon our faith? I have never believed so, at least not until I had ALS. Being diagnosed with a terminal and incurable disease can cause many of your theological predispositions to go out the window. One of the first things I did after I was diagnosed was purchase several books arguing that God wants everyone healed. I wanted to read these books not to argue with their theology but to open-mindedly listen to what they had to say. Because if there was a chance they were right and that my faith could heal me, I would do my best to have that perfect faith.

But over the years, I've realized that a perfect, doubtless faith is not the key to restoring my health.

One of the most interesting stories about healing in the Bible is about a father whose son was possessed by an evil spirit. The father came to Jesus and asked for help. Jesus responded, "Everything is possible for one who believes." The father replied, "I do believe; help me overcome my unbelief!" (Mark 9:23–24). And Jesus healed this father's son. So in at least one case in the Gospels, faith and unbelief coexisted in the same person, and Jesus still gave healing. I like this story. I do believe that God can heal me, even though no one has ever been healed of ALS. I do believe in the power of God to heal. But I have to confess, I also have some reservations and doubts; I am a flawed human being, after all. But I like to believe that, if like this father, my faith is mixed with doubts, yet I ask God to help me with my unbelief, then it is indeed possible for Him to heal me.

Years ago, I decided I wanted someone to anoint me with oil and pray over me for healing. And I wanted someone who actually believed in healing, not someone to pray, "God, heal him if it is Your will." Not that I am opposed to the will of God, but I didn't want someone to pray conditional upon the will of God. I wanted someone to pray, "God, heal him!" So I invited a friend who was pastor of a Pentecostal church here in Grand Rapids to pray for me. He believed in healing. At his church, they had healing services.

It was one of the most moving evenings of my entire life. He began by telling stories of people he had prayed for who were miraculously healed. He also told stories about people he had prayed for who were not healed and had passed away, receiving that ultimate and final healing. Before he prayed for me, he gave me some advice.

"Don't become obsessed with getting healed, Ed," he said. "If you get obsessed, you will lose your focus. Get lost in the wonder of God, and who knows what He will do for you."

This is some of the best advice I have ever received. And he was right; I had become too focused on my own disease and my own future. I needed to shift my focus from myself to my creator. And I shouldn't focus on God's power to heal me, either; I should focus on the all-around wonder of God and spend more time with Him each day without the goal of receiving healing for my good behavior. I needed to trust Him with my life not because I was sick but because I should trust Him that way always.

Since that night, I've been trying to get—and stay—lost in the wonder of God. And it has helped me. I haven't thought much about being miraculously healed lately, although when I do, I still pray for it. But mostly, I simply try to focus on God; sometimes He feels close, and sometimes I can see Him only through a fog. But I know He's there.

In the Bible, there is a story of a blind man in the city of Jericho. He heard that Jesus was passing by in the street, so he began shouting, "Jesus, son of David, have mercy on me!" Jesus called the blind man to Him and ultimately healed him, saying, "Go, your faith has healed you." What faith? It doesn't appear in the story that the blind man had any faith. It certainly doesn't say the blind man was without doubt. Yet apparently his faith was proven to Jesus when he yelled, "Jesus, son of David, have mercy on me!"

Even though I have read this story many times and have preached on it several times, reading it as a man with ALS allowed me to see it anew and inspired me to pray, "Jesus, son of David, have mercy on me." I am not telling God what to do. I am not believing that He will heal me if I am without any doubt. I am not asking God to heal me if it is His will. I am simply throwing myself at His mercy. And just like the blind man, my faith is exercised every time I pray for mercy.

The Bible seems to indicate that there is a vast difference between being cured of a disease and being healed of it. It is possible to be cured, but not healed. And it is possible to be healed, but not cured.

> Now on his way to Jerusalem, Jesus traveled along the border between Samaria and Galilee. As he was going into a village, ten men who had leprosy met him. They stood at a distance and called out in a loud voice, "Jesus, Master, have pity on us!"
>
> When he saw them, he said, "Go, show yourselves to the priests." And as they went, they were cleansed.
>
> One of them, when he saw he was healed, came back, praising God in a loud voice. He threw himself at Jesus' feet and thanked him— and he was a Samaritan.
>
> Jesus asked, "Were not all ten cleansed? Where are the other nine? Has no one returned to give praise to God except this foreigner?" Then he said to him, "Rise and go; your faith has made you well." (Luke 17:11–19)

In this amazing story, we see that all ten lepers were cured. But only one was made well: the one who came back praising God and giving thanks to Jesus. This man was not just cured but also healed.

Another story of healing can be found in the story of Paul.

> Because of these surpassingly great revelations … to keep me from becoming conceited, I was given a thorn in my flesh, a messenger of Satan, to torment me.
>
> Three times I pleaded with the Lord to take it away from me.
>
> But he said to me, "My grace is sufficient for you, for my power is made perfect in weakness."
>
> Therefore I will boast all the more gladly about my weaknesses, so that Christ's power may rest on me.
>
> That is why, for Christ's sake, I delight in weaknesses, in insults, in hardships, in persecutions, in difficulties. For when I am weak, then I am strong. (2 Corinthians 12:7–10)

We do not know what this "thorn" in Paul's flesh was, but it was likely a physical infirmity of some kind. After praying for healing and not receiving it, Paul's ultimate response was that he would be glad about this weakness so that Christ's power might rest on him. So Paul was not cured, but he was healed. He found that God's grace was sufficient to face all of the difficulties and trials of life, and therefore he welcomed such challenges. Incredible! I have discovered that God's grace is sufficient for each new day. But I am not to the point where Paul was; I don't delight in ALS. I don't delight in muscles that quit working. I don't delight in needing help to get dressed. But I read Paul's story and am inspired to keep looking for that strength, to open myself completely to God's grace and allow it to lessen the burden of my disease.

So really, would I rather be healed or be cured? Considering the stories of the lepers and of Paul, I do believe that I have experienced the healing of God. Like the one leper, I give praise to God and thank Jesus for each new day I am given. Like Paul, I have discovered God's grace to be sufficient, even in the face of ALS.

But I still have many, many days when I would much rather be cured.

LIMITATIONS OF HUMAN FLESH

Jesus, though He was God, came into the world in human flesh. Consider the words of the apostle Paul.

Who, being in very nature God,
did not consider equality with God
    something to be used to his own
    advantage;
rather, he made himself nothing
by taking the very nature of a servant,
being made in human likeness.
And being found in appearance as a
    man,
he humbled himself
by becoming obedient to death—
even death on a cross! (Philippians
    2:6–8)

We know from the opening of the gospel of John that Jesus was involved in the creation of the world. He was and is God of every god. So how do you lay aside your

>

What then, really, is healing?

If it is possible to be cured and not healed like the lepers, and if it is possible to be healed but not cured like Paul, then what is healing?

From a biblical perspective, healing is first being at peace with God.

> Therefore, since we have been justified through
> faith, we have peace with God through our Lord
> Jesus Christ. (Romans 5:1)

I first made my peace with God as an eleven-year-old boy in Northern Ireland. It was a Sunday night, and earlier in the day my father had preached on the importance of accepting Jesus as your Savior. After dinner, I went up to my bedroom, which overlooked the backyard. I remember kneeling by my bed, close to the window, and praying to receive

glory and live with the limitations of human flesh? The answer is, I don't know! But I know that He did it. If you were God with all the powers of deity, how would you like to live with the limitations of human flesh? It had to be frustrating. But He did it. Whenever I get frustrated with the fact that more of my muscles don't work, I think of Jesus. It doesn't lessen the limitations in any way, but it does encourage me. Jesus knew the limitations of living His life in the flesh. And if He did that, I can do this too.

Jesus as my Savior and Lord. That was the beginning of my lifelong journey of following Jesus. So am I afraid to die? Absolutely not. I know where I am going. To be absent from this physical body is to be present with the Lord.

The second aspect of healing is to live at peace with others. The Bible says that as much as is possible, live at peace with all people. There is great liberation in being at peace with others. There is a feeling of relief. This is why both asking for and granting forgiveness is so important; it is the key to finding peace with one another.

The final element needed for healing is being at peace with yourself and your circumstances. In the book of Philippians, Paul commended the church for their generous gift. But he reminded them that he did not need it. "I am not saying this because I am in need, for I have learned to be content whatever the circumstances" (Philippians 4:11). Paul was at peace with the circumstances surrounding his life as a Christian. It didn't matter whether he had a lot or very little; he had learned to be content. In the same way, he had learned to be content with that thorn in his flesh. The same is true for my life with ALS. Since I don't know what causes it and since there is no cure, I must learn to be content. I must learn to be at peace. There is no other way. Of course this is often much easier said than done.

So we see healing is made up of finding peace in three areas of life: with God, with others, and with yourself and your circumstances. This is very similar to the definition of the Hebrew word *shalom*, which would substitute the word *wholeness* for *peace*. Shalom is wholeness with God, with others, and with yourself.

When we are whole in those areas, we are also at peace; we can experience a state of total well-being. If you were to go to Jerusalem today, and you wanted to say hello to someone, you would say "Shalom." And if you wanted to say good-bye, you would say the same word. Shalom is the beginning and end of every conversation. In the same way, when it comes to healing, it is the beginning of the process and also the end goal.

There are moments every day when I am at peace, and then there are moments when I am not. Every day is like this, and I suppose it would be regardless of whether or not I had ALS; that's life. But so far I have found that the longer I have this disease, the more I am at peace with it. I pray every day that my moments of worry and frustration will be lessened. I pray every day that my moments of peace would be increased. Each day I pray for mercy and for wholeness.

I want *shalom* in my life.

Of course I would like to be cured. Who wouldn't? But the truth is, I desperately need the healing of God in my life. I know that the grace of God is sufficient for every day, and years into the disease, I testify to His faithfulness.

I'M STILL LIVING

Almost every week these days, I meet with someone who has been recently diagnosed with ALS. We always discuss the disease, the person's diagnosis, and life with ALS. Most people end up asking me, "How have you managed to live this long?"

Honestly, I don't really know how I am still alive and still able to do so much. But I do think there are some things people can do to help themselves when they are diagnosed with any terminal illness. First of all, you need to reduce the stress in your life. Second, you need to quit your job. Third, you need to learn how not to worry about tomorrow. Fourth, you need to learn to be forgiving. Fifth, you need to learn how to be thankful. Those are the big things to strive for. However, there are other things I have found to make a difference in my life.

LAUGHTER

A cheerful heart is good medicine,
but a crushed spirit dries up the bones. (Proverbs
17:22)

When you have ALS, there is very little to laugh about. The future, at best, is uncertain. Every day you must deal with muscles that quit working. You have to adjust everything you do, from eating to walking to driving to brushing your teeth to putting on your clothes. So it is hard to laugh. But not impossible.

Many years ago, I read a book by a medical doctor who was in the hospital as a patient. His condition was serious, and he had terrible pain. One day he was watching *The Three Stooges* on the television, and he noticed that when he was laughing, his pain subsided. In fact, it went away completely for the moment. So this doctor began a journey on which he cured himself by laughing out loud. I know, it sounds crazy. But what did I have to lose? I began watching *The Three Stooges*, and I laughed and laughed during each episode. I didn't have pain to be eased by laughter, but I did feel a lot better.

Have you ever heard the story about the Irishman who emigrated from Dublin and was living in Boston? He went into the pub, sat on the barstool, and ordered five pints of Guinness. He returned to the pub the same time the following week and ordered five pints of Guinness. This went on for several months. Same time. Same day of the week. Same five pints of Guinness. After a while the bartender became curious. "You come in here the same time, the same day, and you always order five pints of Guinness. Why?"

"Back in Dublin, on this day and at this time every week, I used to meet my four friends for a round of Guinness. So now I come here each week and I drink a pint of Guinness for me and four pints to remember my friends."

The man continued coming to the pub each week for about a year. Then one day, he came in and ordered only four pints of Guinness. For the next month he did the same. The bartender was curious again. "You used to order five pints of Guinness. Now you only order four. Has one of your friends passed away?"

"Not at all. I've given up drinking for Lent."

Every time I think about that story I laugh. I love funny movies. I love *The Three Stooges*. And the more I laugh, the better I feel.

DIET

Shortly after I was diagnosed with ALS, I was driving down the road and pulled up to a stoplight. The person who pulled up next to me was a friend who attended Calvary Church. We waved to each other. Later that day he called me.

"I was so glad I pulled up next to you today. You have been on my mind. I have a friend who is a scientist. He works with doctors in helping them with nutrition for their patients. He's worked with professional athletes, politicians, and other famous people. He's worked with doctors all over the country. Would you be willing to have him analyze your blood? He would then make recommendations for vitamins, supplements, and your diet."

"I'd be delighted. Can you set that up?"

So I had my blood work done, and the doctor sent me a detailed memo that included vitamins, supplements, and recommendations for my diet. His overall advice was, "Your job is to live as healthily as possible. If you do that, who knows what God might do." The vitamins and supplements were not a problem to incorporate into my daily life. The diet, however, was a huge challenge. The doctor recommended that I go gluten-free. This was eleven years ago, and back then there were very few options for a gluten-free diet. He also recommended that I stop consuming dairy products, sugar, and caffeine. My wife wanted to be supportive and partner with me by changing her diet as well, but after the first night she said that her goal was to have the next meal. Beyond that, she wasn't sure she could keep doing it. After all, these were radical changes to make overnight.

So how in the world could I make such sweeping changes? With no cure for ALS, I figured I might as well try anything. I kept to this diet for the next three years. I followed the doctor's advice as closely as possible. And do you know what? I was healthier for those three years than I have ever been in my life. I put on weight. My allergies did not bother me. I used to get frequent colds and sore throats, but during those three years, I was never sick. About a year into eating this way, I told the doctor at the ALS clinic, "If this disease gets me, it will get the healthiest person it has ever gotten." We both laughed.

Months later, I was in an online chat room for ALS patients. I was talking to a guy in West Virginia, telling him that I was eating gluten-free and avoiding milk products, sugar, and coffee. He said, "I do the opposite. I eat ice cream. I smoke cigarettes. I drink beer every day. I drink lots of coffee. I figure that this disease is going to get me in the end, so I am living every day to its fullest. So I eat what I want and I drink what I want. It is fine for you to eat the way you do, but for me, I want to enjoy the time I have left." I had to admit, that was not bad advice and that man certainly had a point.

Over a year later, I did go off the diet.

But from time to time I go back on.

Sometimes, I suppose, I want to enjoy life like my friend from West Virginia. And sometimes I want to try anything that can help me stick around longer.

MAGNETS

Shortly before I was diagnosed, my wife found great help for some back issues she had been having, in the form of magnets. Since they worked so well for her, I decided to try them as well. I have a magnet necklace around my neck, and I wear bracelets that have magnets. Do they help? Honestly, I don't know. But I have been wearing them since I was diagnosed with ALS. And I won't go without them.

PURIFIED WATER AND AIR

Water is critical, no matter what your situation. My house now has a water-purification system that also magnetizes the water. I try to drink six to eight glasses of water a day. I know, that is a lot of drinking and also a lot of going to the bathroom.

We also have air purifiers in several rooms. I figure the quality of the air we breathe and the water we drink is important. This belief is reinforced when I see the dirty air filters when my wife replaces them! I would hate to do without the air purifiers and the water purifier.

PRAYER

I am blessed to say that there are many hundreds of people who pray for me every day. Am I still alive because of their prayers? I don't know. Does God operate on the idea that the more people who pray for you, the more you are healed? I do not think so. But I am really grateful so many people pray for me. I think I am still alive, in part, as an answer to their prayers. But how much prayer influences my length of life, I cannot say.

12

GOD IN THE PAST, PRESENT, AND FUTURE

When you know you are dying, you begin reflecting not only on the past but also on the present and the future. And when you are a Christian, your reflection probably includes the role of God in your past, present, and future.

So where is God? God has promised that in each moment of life His grace will be sufficient. Where is that grace? Sure, it's relatively easy to see God and His grace in the past; after all, hindsight is 20/20. But it's not so easy to see God in the present. And it's almost impossible to see God and His grace in the future.

THE PAST

I grew up in a working-class neighborhood in Belfast, Northern Ireland. Before my father became a pastor, he delivered bread for a local bread company. His bread route went right past our house.

One day, when I was just a boy, my father stopped for lunch at the house. In those days he delivered the bread with a horse and carriage. While my father was eating in the house, I went outside to talk with the horse. I said to the horse, "Giddyap. Giddyap." And shock of shocks, the horse took off and went around the corner!

I didn't follow the horse. I thought I would stay there until my father came out. I knew I was in deep trouble. When my father came out, he said, "Where's my horse?"

I said, "Actually, I think I'm to blame. I talked to him, and he took off." So he walked after the horse.

Fortunately for me, the horse had just gone to the next customer on the bread route.

Eventually my dad became a pastor at a church. We went to church every Sunday morning as well as stayed for the breaking of the bread (Communion). We would then go back in the afternoon for Sunday school and back again at night for the gospel meeting. We also attended several services during the week. So church has always been an important part of my life. My dad did not have an office at the church. Rather, he had a study in our home. Even though he studied several days a week, he always had time for us kids. Many times I would be out playing football (soccer) in the street, and my dad would be studying for a sermon. Hearing us outside, he would quit studying for the sermon and join us on the street playing football. This happened many times over. I realized my dad was more interested in me than he was in preparing his sermons.

Not that everything was perfect growing up. One time, I was walking back from speech lessons and it was snowing, which was very rare in Belfast. Most of the doors on the neighborhood houses were stained glass. I don't know what possessed me, but I made a snowball and threw it at a stained-glass door. The next thing I heard was glass shattering, so I took off running. The owner of the house came out and began chasing me. I don't know what I was thinking, but I ran around the back of my own house and hid. I waited for quite a while before I went into the house. When I slowly entered through the back door and went into the kitchen area, I noticed all the lights were out. Then I realized that my dad was standing there. He was not happy. I ended up paying for the stained-glass door, and my activities were limited for a long time.

When we came to the United States, I went through a battery of tests at the public high school to determine which grade I should enter. Judging just by my age, I would've belonged in the ninth grade, but since the curriculum in Belfast differed from what American students experienced, I was matched according to what I had learned. The school told my dad I could go into ninth, tenth, eleventh, or twelfth grade, or I could begin college. My dad chose to enroll me in the eleventh grade. So I skipped two grades and ended up graduating when I was sixteen.

Since I was brand-new in America, the school assigned another guy to help me get adjusted. His name was Joe Theismann. He played on the football team as the quarterback. Joe went on to play at Notre Dame, in the Canadian football league, and finally in the NFL.

I remember I was somewhat embarrassed by my thick accent. Many times at school, I would be surrounded by a group of girls saying, "Talk to us." I decided early on that I would do everything I could to speak American—not Irish. I understand this is probably not the decision most teenage boys would make, given the attention I received as a result of my accent!

Despite my initial plans to the contrary, I ended up staying at Bob Jones University. And, as I mentioned before, I earned both a bachelor's degree and a master's degree there. When I was in graduate school, I met my wife, who was a senior at the university. We began dating, and the truth is, I fell head over heels in love with her right away. When we both graduated, we married.

I wrote letters to three hundred churches, announcing that I was becoming an evangelist and asking if they would like me to come preach. But none of them wrote back.

Eventually, though, I landed that great job working with Jerry Falwell at Lynchburg Baptist College (Liberty University) in Virginia. I was set up pretty nice for a while, and then Jerry asked me if I would go over to Buena Vista to start a church. A number of people from that city rode the bus over the mountain to Thomas Road Baptist Church every Sunday, and they really wanted to start their own church. I agreed to go and started the church in an elementary school cafeteria. In the beginning, we had thirty-three people. Two years later, we had over three hundred regular attenders. This is where I fell in love with preaching. Not just preaching, but preaching to the same people week after week and getting to know them. When I think about that church, I see in my mind all sorts of different people.

As pastor, I had an agreement that I would go visit anybody at any time. One of the men asked me to visit his dad. I quickly agreed. Then he told me his dad was the leading bootlegger in the whole county and would probably meet me at the door with a shotgun to get me off the property. But I had agreed to go, so I walked up to the door, rang the doorbell, and prayed they would not be home. His wife came to the door, and I introduced myself. She said to come on in. We went to the back porch of the house at the foot of the Blue Ridge mountains. I met the dad—his name was Mr. Camden—and he had the hardest, coldest look on his face. We sat down and talked, and at the end of the conversation, I read from the Bible and gave a brief "plan of salvation." As I closed in prayer, I asked his wife if she would like to accept Jesus, and she immediately said yes. I led her in a prayer, then turned to Mr. Camden, who had said nothing the whole time, and asked him if he would like to accept Jesus. He began to cry. Then he sobbed. And we got down on our knees together, and he invited Jesus into his life.

The next week, he took me to meet all of his bootlegging customers. He said, "This man changed my life. He'll change yours. Now, have at it."

I later baptized Mr. Camden in a nearby river. On one Sunday over fifty members of his family were in church. I learned the power of the gospel to radically transform a person's life. Seeing people's lives changed helped me understand that ministry was more than just preaching.

Eventually, I settled into ministry at Liberty University and Thomas Road Baptist Church. I was enjoying life in Virginia and never forgot to thank God for guiding me there. But after nearly fifteen years working with Jerry Falwell, I started to feel God was leading me to make a change. I felt a call to pastor a church again. Lorna and I prayed about this for more than a year. Then one day Calvary Church in Grand Rapids, Michigan, called me. They wanted me to come for a Sunday and preach. I told them I was not interested in becoming their pastor, but nevertheless I would come and preach. On the Sunday I preached at Calvary Church, the search committee asked if I could meet with them. I agreed to meet with them but honestly had little or no interest in pastoring the church. They had just moved into a brand-new building. At the meeting, the chairman asked, "How do you like our new building?" I answered, "Do you think God is impressed with this building? He created the world in seven days, so do you think He's impressed? A church is not a building. A church is people."

This was my opening statement to the pulpit committee!

But they eventually invited me to come anyway.

I was a bit surprised, but I felt God was calling me out of Lynchburg, where I was involved in a whole variety of jobs, and into a job where I could be just a pastor. Through several months of trips to and from Michigan and Virginia, I met with board members, staff, church members, and the pulpit committee. Gradually my attitude changed and I gained a renewed sense of calling to be a full-time pastor. The church voted to call me in March, and after a brief but desperate feeling of uncertainty, I accepted their call.

So during spring break in 1987, we drove as a family to Grand Rapids in our 1978 Pontiac. I had received the keys to the church, so after I dropped my family off at the hotel, I went up to the church to pray. I opened the front door and walked in. I made my way down to the altar and got down on my knees. "Dear God, please don't let this church go downhill."

I know this was a very selfish prayer. I know this is not the way you're supposed to pray. But this was an honest expression of my heart. The church had about thirteen hundred people in attendance each Sunday. I

REGRETS (WORK)

I don't have a lot of regrets. I have spent my life trying to do what God wants me to do. And I love what I have done. I have tried to live my life by this motto: preach the Bible and love people. I try to do both. As a pastor, I worked hard in sermon preparation and I tried to always love everybody I met. But looking back, I know I worked way too hard.

When I was a pastor, on Saturday nights I would speak at a service for unreached people. I wore jeans and a T-shirt. At the end of my talk, I answered questions directly from the audience. Hundreds of people found Jesus through those services. Then on Sunday mornings, I put on a suit and tie and spoke three times with a completely different message to a completely different audience. Then on Sunday night, I spoke again at another kind of service. That is three different messages in five different services

>

>

within a twenty-four-hour period. Honestly, that was way too much work for one person. Once in a while you could do that. But week after week, month after month, year after year, it gets to be too much. And in addition to sermon preparation and preaching, there were also staff meetings, board meetings, counseling, hospital visitations, funerals, and weddings.

If I had to do it over, I would not have spoken that much or worked that hard. Sometimes there is an expectation in the Lord's church that the senior pastor will do everything. Unfortunately, that's not possible. I don't think I ever took a full vacation in the more than eighteen years I was a pastor. I would often try to take a day off here and there, but many times it was interrupted with a crisis, because of the size of the church. Looking back, I regret working so hard.

didn't want that number to go down after I started there; I wanted the church to grow. When I left almost two decades later, it was running over five thousand regular attenders.

My prayer was answered! But is that how you measure success in church ministry? The sermons preached? The funerals preached? The weddings conducted? The board meetings attended? The people counseled? The crises dealt with? The finances raised? The people baptized? The hospitals visited? I think the answer is all of these and none of these. The real answer is in the lives you touch and the people you influence for Jesus. And that's success whether you are a minister or not.

So as I look back on my journey through life, I have never heard God speak to me directly. I have never heard His voice. But I have seen Him through the actions and compassion of others. I saw Him in the life of my dad. I saw Him in the lives of many people at Bob Jones University. I saw Him in the life of Jerry Falwell and many others. As long as I am trying to live in obedience to Scripture, God extends His grace toward me through people. However, if I am living in disobedience to Scripture, I fail to see His grace in my life.

THE PRESENT

Even though I can see God and His grace in the past, at times it is very difficult to see Him and His grace in the present. In fact, we tend to forget how God has met us in the past. We get so overwhelmed with our present circumstances that we lose all perspective. It's like descending into a fog; what we see clearly in the past is no longer clear, and the road ahead seems so uncertain.

In the past, I discovered God and His grace in the people around me and through studying Scripture. So is this where we find Him in the present also? I think so. However, finding God in the Scriptures can be a bit of a challenge. Once I was diagnosed with ALS, I did not feel like reading the Bible. It was a bit too much for me. But I did find God in the people around me. So where is God when life falls apart? He is there in the people He puts around us.

First and foremost on my list of people in whom I see God and His grace is my wife. Without her, my life would be impossible. Early on I tried to do everything myself. Even if it took me ten minutes to button my shirt, I did it myself. I think I was desperate in those days to do everything myself, so I refused all help. But so many years later, my situation is radically different. My tongue is weak, so it's difficult to move around large amounts of food in my mouth. My fingers don't work well. I have a difficult time writing my signature. I can no longer type on the computer. My arms are weak. My right hand no longer works, and I have always been right-handed. So I now eat with my left hand. But I tire quickly in lifting food to my mouth, so I need help toward the end of the meal in getting the food to my mouth. I can no longer get shirts over my head. Frankly, it's a pain in the neck. But this is exactly where I had discovered God's grace in my life: through my wife. She willingly and enthusiastically helps me do all these things. Without her, my life would be an immense challenge. With her, I am still able to do most things.

Second would be my kids. Whenever I am meeting with them, they are always looking out for me. They are more than willing to help. And then there are my grandkids. The oldest two constantly look out for me. They offer help putting on and taking off coats, and they offer help at the table. And I am more than willing to let them help. The youngest ones keep me laughing. They are God's grace when I need it most. They are the presence of God in my life.

In addition to my family, I also have an accountability group of men at Calvary Church. Early on they met with me and spent several hours praying for healing. In those early days they were my lifeline to God. They loved me. They helped me. They prayed for me. They encouraged me. They uplifted me. They were my hope.

And there have been many other people in my life as well. People who have prayed for me. People who have encouraged me. People who have helped me financially. And then there was the church. When I was thinking of retiring, they encouraged me to go see a financial planner. They provided me with a comfortable living after I resigned from the church. And they have not forgotten about me. Six years later, they are still concerned; they meet with and pray regularly for me. I am so glad God brought me to Calvary Church. They have been God's hands and feet in my life.

THE FUTURE

After eleven years with ALS, I have learned to try not to think about the future. I try to live every day to the fullest and enjoy it. But in the back of my mind, I am still worried about what's to come. It is like my shadow; it always follows me around. Even in the brightest of days, it's always there. So what about the future? I have set three goals for myself for my future. First, I want to speak for as long as I can. Second, when I can no longer speak, I want to write as long as I can. Third, when I can no longer speak or write, I want to live as long as I can. That's it. Those are my goals.

When I was pastor at Calvary Church, I encouraged the congregation to read through the Bible every year. In retrospect, this was one of the most important things I have done in ministry. It exposed thousands of people to the Bible on a daily basis. Every week in the bulletin, we would print the scripture for the coming week. The week I was diagnosed with ALS, we were reading the 38th chapter of the book of Isaiah. This is the story of how the prophet Isaiah was commanded by God to go to King Hezekiah and tell him to put his house in order because he was going to die. Upon hearing this request, the king wept bitterly. He prayed to God, and God changed His mind. He told Isaiah that because of Hezekiah's prayers, God would add fifteen years to Hezekiah's life.

This is a great story. But what did it mean for me, having just been diagnosed with ALS? Would God add fifteen more years to my life if I asked Him to? Was God speaking directly to me through His Word? Or was it just coincidence that I was reading this story the week I was diagnosed? These are still compelling questions for me to this day.

Back then, had you told me I would have fifteen more years to live, I would have been happy. Now that it's been over eleven years, I find myself greedy for more time. I want more than four more years. The first year I was diagnosed, a woman in our church prayed that I would have fifteen more years. The second year after I was diagnosed, she prayed for fifteen more years. And the following year, she again prayed for fifteen more years. Every year, she prays that I will have fifteen more years. I sure hope her prayers are granted.

Like I said, I want to speak as long as I can. I know the day will come when I can no longer speak. Even now, my speaking is much slower than it used to be.

When I was a pastor, I would try to have all of my sermon preparation done by noon on Wednesday. Then I would have the rest of the week to think through illustrations. Many of those illustrations came to me while I was running in the afternoons at the indoor track. However, every once in a rare while, I would think of a better illustration while I was preaching. About a year after I was diagnosed, I was preaching one Sunday on giving. I was teaching from 2 Corinthians about generosity: "And they did not do as we expected, but they gave themselves first to the Lord and then to us in keeping with God's will" (2 Corinthians 8:5). As I spoke, I realized we had just received the offering prior to the start of the sermon. And it dawned on me. I asked one of the ushers to bring me an offering plate. I told the congregation that when the offering plate was passed a few moments ago, they should have stood up and gotten in the offering plate. The usher brought the offering plate, and for the rest of the sermon, I stood in the offering plate and spoke.

I asked the congregation, "What are you holding back from the offering plate? What areas of your life need to get into the offering plate?" Walking alone down the back hallway after the last service, I began asking myself, *What am I holding back from the offering plate? What areas of my life need to get into the plate?* Then I realized that my speaking and preaching should be in the offering plate. I can take you to the very place in that back hallway where I put those things in the offering plate for God. I prayed, "I am now surrendering my speaking and preaching to You. I'm putting it in the offering plate. If the day comes when I can no longer speak or preach, I want You to know that it's okay with me." Several days later, one of the Sunday school classes gave me a photo of me standing in the offering plate. At the bottom of the photo were the words my dad often spoke to me: "You are indispensable until your work on earth is done." I still have that photo in my study. It reminds me every day that my work here isn't done. It also reminds me of the moment when I gave my speaking and preaching ability to God.

I've written a lot of books over the years. When I first started writing, I wrote everything out in longhand on a yellow legal pad. When I had finished writing out the book, I would have an assistant type up the manuscript on a typewriter. This was long before computers. But even when I had a computer, I would still write the manuscript out longhand on a legal pad and have an assistant type it on the computer. Eventually I did type the manuscript myself, but it took me a while to make the adjustment.

However, as ALS began to impact my fingers, I found it increasingly difficult to type, and eventually I was unable to type at all. Now I use a voice-activated system. So I have gone from writing the manuscript out longhand to typing it to speaking into a computer and letting the computer type it for me. I'm not sure what I will do when I can no longer speak, except live as long as I can.

Early on, the doctors who diagnosed me told me I needed to make decisions about feeding tubes, breathing assistance, and ventilators. Right now my decision is to be open to a feeding tube and breathing assistance. But I am not interested in being on a ventilator at this time. While a ventilator significantly extends life, what kind of life is it? And what about the people who will have to take care of me then? These are complicated decisions to make, and even this far into the disease, sometimes I feel powerless to make them. And perhaps that's okay.

When it comes to the future, I am praying that the grace God has shown me in the past and in the present will continue to see me through. My future is really uncertain, and given what I know about ALS, it looks pretty bleak. I am grateful for the eleven years I have had so far, but I also know that every year I have left will be increasingly unpleasant.

So what can I say of God and His grace in the future? The reality is that God has brought me this far. As I look back on my life, I am fully aware of the presence of God and of His grace. Every day is a gift. Every day I am trusting in God and in His grace. Every day I try to live life to its fullest. I try not to worry about tomorrow. I try to focus on today. And I know that God and His grace are sufficient for the moment I find myself in.

When I wake up tomorrow, whatever the challenges, I know God will be there and will provide His grace. This is my hope. This is my strength.

13

HEAVEN

When I was first diagnosed with ALS, many people often said to me, "I bet you're thinking a lot about heaven." My reply was always the same: "I have not been thinking about heaven at all. I have discovered how attached I am to my family and my friends. The last thing I want to think about is heaven." That was eleven years ago. Now I am beginning to think about life after death. After all, the closer you get to death, the more natural it is to think about it.

When I was growing up, a popular evangelism question was "If you were to die in the next five minutes, do you know for sure that you would go to heaven?" While this is certainly a legitimate question, following Jesus is supposed to be about a lot more than just getting into heaven; most of the Bible deals with living life in the present, not with where we go after we die. Yet humanity has always been obsessed with thoughts of the afterlife. So, what is heaven like?

It's about the family of God.

> Do not let your hearts be troubled. You believe
> in God; believe also in me. My Father's house has
> many rooms; if that were not so, would I have
> told you that I am going there to prepare a place
> for you? And if I go and prepare a place for you,
> I will come back and take you to be with me that
> you also may be where I am. (John 14:1–3)

Jesus said these words as He was about to enjoy the Last Supper with His disciples. He told them that He was going away and that they were not to worry. He was going away to prepare a place for them, which meant He would come back and get them.

The Greek word in this verse for "place" actually translates to *room*. In the Jewish tradition of the time, parents negotiated marriage contracts on behalf of their children. When the covenant was signed, the boy would return to his father's house to add an extra room for his bride. When the room was finished, the marriage ceremony would be completed. The couple would move in together into the father's house. This is what Jesus was talking about in these verses. Just like the groom, He went away to prepare a room, a place, for us. When He is finished, He will come and get us.

But where exactly is this place Jesus is preparing? Many Christians believe that if you could go to the farthest end of the universe, beyond that is heaven. In other words, when you get to the end of the universe, you have reached the beginning of heaven. For many years, I believed that to be true.

But then I was reading the account of the first documented Christian martyr, Stephen. When he was about to die, Stephen said that he saw heaven open up and Jesus standing at the right hand of God. Did he actually see to the farthest end of the universe? Did he have super vision that could transcend the universe? Or was heaven around him and in a dimension he could not see, taste, or touch? As Stephen was about to die, did God open up that dimension for him? I am now inclined to believe that heaven is right around us. We cannot see it. We cannot taste it. We cannot touch it. It is in a dimension that is beyond us and surrounds us. Regardless of where heaven is, it does exist; it is a "place." It is a real place, for real people, forever.

So what is heaven like? In the book of Revelation, John described the New Jerusalem. He talked about a new heaven and a new earth coming into existence. He stated that when this happens "there will be no more death or mourning or crying or pain, for the old order of things has passed away" (Revelation 21:4). No more gathering at the graveside. No more sorrow. No more pain. No more ALS. No more cancer. No more divorce. After all, the old order of things (the here and now) has been replaced with a new order of things. Thank God, it will be a new day.

My dad, who is now in heaven, used to say that there are three words that describe heaven: *better by far*. In the book of Philippians, Paul struggled with the idea of wanting to go and be with Christ, yet he knew his responsibilities in the present moment were great. So he was torn between the two. Of his longing to go and be with Christ, Paul stated that to do so would be "better by far" than what life on earth can be (Philippians 1:23). Those three words always stuck with my dad, and when my mother died, he put it on her gravestone. So what is heaven like? You can take the absolute best of what we do down here and yet heaven is better by far.

I was with my mom when she died. The last week, I told her I would be with her twenty-four hours a day. She said to me, "Get my coat." And I said, "Mom, you're in the hospital. You don't need a coat." She said, "Get my coat." I said, "Why do you need a coat?" She answered, "Wilma is out in the hall and wants to meet me." Wilma had passed away a month earlier of cancer. She and my mom had become the best of friends. I think, toward the end, she was more heaven-focused than earth-focused. I read in the hospice material that that often happens. People start talking about people who've gone on before. And my mom was alert the same day. My dad, who was diabetic, couldn't find the machine to test his blood, and my mom said, "Look in your hand!" and my dad was holding it. So she wasn't delirious or heavy on drugs. She was just thinking about heaven.

So if heaven is so wonderful, why aren't we demanding to go there? Why do I want so badly to be cured and to live for decades yet on this earth? Such questions are frequently on my mind. Living with ALS, with a constant reminder that my time here is limited, has made me realize how attached I am to my wife, my kids, my grandkids, and my friends. Maybe one day soon I'll be longing for heaven. But for right now, I am hoping I can stay here for quite a while longer.

Whenever I think of "the best" down here on earth, I don't think of the sermons I have preached or the weddings and funerals I have conducted. I think of the best times I've had with my family. I think of the time when I took them all back to Northern Ireland, when the children were old enough to understand where we were. We stayed in a hotel on the north coast. It was across the road from an oceanside golf course. The wind was blowing, and it was raining almost constantly, yet people continued to golf. On several occasions during our visit, my family would sit together and watch people play from our hotel room. The harsh weather caused people to lean heavily into the wind then to run together to the next shot, which rarely seemed to stay on the fairway. We laughed and laughed at them.

After watching them for a few days, finally we decided to go and play. The wind was blowing off the ocean. So wouldn't you know, whenever we hit the ball, we would have to lean into the wind. And it was so cold, we would run between shots. What we had laughed at in others we were now doing ourselves!

I am so blessed to have so many wonderful memories with my family. Fly-fishing with the kids each summer. Evening walks with Lorna and the dog after all our children had left for college. Eating meals together at holidays, or any day. Laughing together and telling stories. Sitting on the porch together as the sun set and the fireflies came out. So what is heaven like? It's all the wonder and joy of the here and now. Except, it's better by far.

REFLECTION GUIDE

INTRODUCTION

Whether you are facing your own struggles or you are walking with someone who is struggling, this book is for you. Ed's stories have provided hope and strength for the people who have known him and who have come to know his life through the film series *Ed's Story*. And even though sometimes there aren't easy answers, scriptures, or prayers, we can still find hope and strength in the questions and in crying out to God.

As you go through this guide, free yourself to ask difficult questions about your life and about God, and begin to search for God even in the midst of the fog. As Jacob said in Genesis 28:16, "Surely the LORD is in this place—and I did not know it!" (NRSV).

CHAPTER 1: THE DIAGNOSIS

1. When do you remember something first being or feeling physically wrong?

   How did you react?

   Had you known anyone who had gone through something like this, or were you the first in your experience?

2. Have you struggled with the thought that Ed shares: "The easiest thing would be to lie down ... and just wait for death"?

   What has kept you from giving up?

3. Even if you have decided not to give up, you may still feel like you have been buried alive. After receiving the diagnosis of "probable ALS," Ed drove home and called his children. Have you had these types of conversations with family?

   How did those conversations make you feel?

4. Ed describes the day after his diagnosis as the first day of the rest of his life. Can you relate?

5. Spend a few moments in silence, meditating on the beginning of your struggles and how your life changed in those moments. Become aware of how you perceive those memories, and ask God for a divine perspective, for the wisdom to find redemption even in this difficult time.

CHAPTER 2: THE FOG

1. "There was a great disparity between my theological knowledge and my personal experience." Do you resonate with Ed's words about the gap between faith and experience?

   What kinds of things do you struggle to believe in the midst of suffering?

   Have you found any answers for these doubts?

2. Ed recalls his memories of Thanksgivings before and after he was diagnosed with ALS. How has your suffering transformed family time and holidays?

   Have you tried to put up a brave front like Ed did, or was your experience more visceral?

3. Jesus was "familiar with pain" according to the prophet Isaiah. What does this mean for you?

4. Take a few moments to embrace the daily struggle to experience what you believe and to choose to live instead of to die. Thank God for another day.

CHAPTER 3: CONNECTING WITH OTHERS

1. Have you met others who are struggling or suffering as you are or have?

    What has meeting those people meant to you?

    Do you find that being with them brings you life or drains you of energy?

2. What does Ed mean that there is power in two broken people talking?

3. Think about the people you have met because of your suffering. Thank God for them, and ask God to open your eyes to the blessing of their friendship. Remember, you aren't agreeing that it was worth it to suffer simply to express gratitude for the relationships that came as a result.

CHAPTER 4: PASTOR NO MORE

1. Have you ever sought God's will in strange ways similar to Ed's random opening of his Bible?

2. Have you had to give up something as a result of your suffering?
    How did it feel?
    Do you miss it?
    Have you found something to take its place?

3. Take a moment to meditate on the things you have lost as a result of your suffering. Grieve if you can. Thank God for them. And ask God for the strength to see hope for what lies ahead.

CHAPTER 5: A YEAR OF LIVING LIKE JESUS

1. Ed's year is chronicled in the book *The Year of Living Like Jesus*. Have you done anything in the midst of your suffering that is something you wouldn't have attempted before?

   What was the result?

2. Ed found that his project kept his mind off the disease. What kinds of things distract you from your suffering? Reflect on those experiences.

3. Consider giving yourself a project that could last a month or longer. Does it excite you?

   Does it scare you?

   Who could join you in this project? Or perhaps your project will be to simply sit and rest and be present in the moment. Thank God for the gift of hope, no matter what you decide to do with the next month or so.

CHAPTER 6: GIVING THANKS

1. In discussing gratefulness, Ed reminds us that the Scriptures say, "In everything give thanks." How does it change your view of God to consider that you do not need to be grateful for your suffering but that you can give thanks in the midst of your suffering?

2. Ed made a list of things he was thankful for. Make your own list. Ask others to help you make your list if it is too difficult. Thank God for everything on your list, and feel free to add to the list later. If it helps, also make a list of things you aren't grateful for. It's okay to grieve the presence of things in your life that aren't good. But then go back to the things that are good, and thank God for them again.

CHAPTER 7: WHEN GOD IS SILENT

1. Have you ever been present while someone is praying for you?

    Did the prayer work?

    What does it mean for prayer to work?

2. Ed recounts several occasions when his wife, Lorna, spoke truth to him. Do you have someone who is willing to speak truth into your life in the midst of your suffering?

    Are you able to hear it?

3. Ed says that the Corvette was never really his, but he drove it for a while. Have you lost anyone in this journey through the "fog"?

    Will someone eventually lose you?

    What could you do with that person that you would later remember like Ed and J. J.'s trip across the country?

4. Ed postulates that Jesus felt abandoned by God on the cross as He experienced His full humanity. Does this give you hope as well?

What do Jesus's words on the cross mean for you?

5. Consider how God acts and speaks through the people around you. Even when God is silent, He can be found in the people around you and in the love you share. Take a moment to think about how you can be more aware of God's love in the love you share with others. Remind yourself that in the presence of others, God is there in the midst.

CHAPTER 8: FORGIVENESS

1. Have you ever had someone ask you for forgiveness?

   How did you react?

   Do you wish you had done anything differently?

2. Have you ever asked forgiveness from someone?

   How did that person react?

3. Are there people of whom you need to ask forgiveness?

   Will you make a list?

   Can you ask forgiveness from each of them?

   What barriers or hesitancies do you feel to accomplishing this list?

   What do you think will be the result of each encounter?

4. Take a moment to meditate on the nature of forgiveness. What does it mean that God has forgiven you?

What does it mean that you can forgive others and be forgiven by them? Thank God for forgiveness and grace.

CHAPTER 9: WORRY

1. Do you find that it is easy to worry about tomorrow?

   What do you think Jesus meant when He said not to worry?

   What were His hearers most worried about?

   What do you worry most about?

2. Spend a few moments writing down your worries, praying about them, and letting them go. Write down any words of hope from Scripture or elsewhere and place them in a location where you will read them often.

CHAPTER 10: HEALING

1. What have you thought about healing during your suffering?

2. Ed wants to believe that he can be healed but doesn't think it's about his faith. What do you think about a God who would require you to have the perfect faith to be healed?

   What do you think it would take for you to be delivered from your suffering?

3. Ed chose to get lost in the wonder of God and pray for mercy. Will you be able to do the same?

4. How does Ed's explanation of *shalom* help you in your struggles?

   Can you envision what it will be like to have peace with God, with others, and with your circumstances?

5. Ask God to heal you—not just to deliver you from circumstances. Write down what it would mean for you to see healing

in your life. And thank God that healing and redemption are available to you today.

CHAPTER 11: I'M STILL LIVING

1. Take the time to consider your diet, environment, and prayer life. How can you live through these things as Ed is living through them?

2. Has laughter been a healing medicine in your experience? What makes you laugh?

CHAPTER 12: GOD IN THE PAST, PRESENT, AND FUTURE

1. As you read about Ed's past, think about your life so far. Where is God in your past?

   Can you point to instances of the sacred in the midst of your life?

   Has God been there all along?

2. Ed admits it's harder to find God in the everyday present than in the past. Can you find those same moments of sacred space as you are living them out?

3. The future may be the hardest thing to think about. But the future is your opportunity to speak your surrender to God, to think about what might come and how you can receive it as a gift. The future is what holds the outworking of hope. What grace do you expect to find in the future?

How can you trust that the future will hold grace from God?

How can you approach the future with a heart filled with life?

CHAPTER 13: HEAVEN

1. Did you grow up with the question "If you were to die tonight, do you know for sure you would go to heaven?"

    How have you answered that question through the years?

2. Ed is inclined to believe that heaven is all around us. What do you think?

3. What does "better by far" mean to you?

    How can you get there?

4. Thank God for the heaven that you find all around you. And consider how to take full advantage of that heaven while you can.

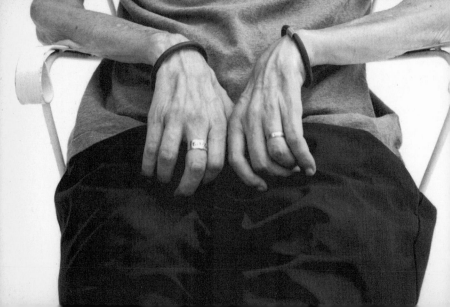

IT AIN'T OVER
TIL IT'S OVER

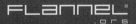
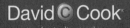